RTI Strategies for All Teachers

Adapted from

by Corwin Press

Presented by

Susan Fitzell M. Ed.

www.SusanFitzell.com

sfitzell@SusanFitzell.com

If you have questions or would like customized school in-service or ongoing consultation, contact:
Susan Gingras Fitzell
PO Box 6182
Manchester, NH 03108-6182
Phone: 603-625-6087 or 210-473-2863
Email: SFitzell@SusanFitzell.com

Main Website: http://www.SusanFitzell.com
Interactive Blog & Teacher Resource: http://www.HighTestScores.org
Interactive Blog & Teacher Resource: http://responsetointerventiononline.com
Facebook: http://www.facebook.com/SusanFitzellfb
YouTube: http://www.youtube.com/susanfitzell
Twitter: http://twitter.com/susanfitzell
For supplemental handouts and information:
www.aimhieducational.com/inclusion.aspx

Other selected titles by Susan Gingras Fitzell, M.Ed.:

Special Needs In The General Classroom: Strategies That Make It Work

Paraprofessionals and Teachers Working Together

Umm Studying? What's That?: Learning Strategies for the Overwhelmed and Confused College and High School Student

Please Help Me With My Homework! Strategies for Parents and Caregivers

Transforming Anger to Personal Power: An Anger Management Curriculum for Grades 6 through 12

Free the Children: Conflict Education for Strong & Peaceful Minds

For more products by Susan visit www.CogentCatalyst.com

Table of Contents and Chapter Descriptions.

Part 1: Introduction

A. Multi-Tier System of Supports
MTSS
(another name for RTI)

B. RTI - Really Terrific
Instruction

C. RTI is ① Research Based
② Frequent Assessments
③ Problem Solving

Response
to
Intervention

TARGETED
INTERVENTIONS

Intensify, Increase
frequency & time:

Memory Strategies

DIFFERENTIATED
TEACHING

HIGH QUALITY
INSTRUCTION

Response to Intervention at the Classroom Level: Introduction

The purpose of this book is to alleviate classroom teachers' stress and confusion regarding RTI at the Classroom level by providing practical, research-based strategies for intervention from Tier One through Tier Three. Response to Intervention is, in a sense, a misnomer. It should be called, "responding to the struggling learner with academic interventions that match the student's needs." These interventions are chosen from researched based strategies and, as a result of a problem solving process, are frequently monitored and adjusted as necessary.

The most important concept to take away is: Response to Intervention is simply 'really good teaching.'

The Three Tiers (Sometimes Four)

"RTI is the practice of providing high quality instruction/intervention matched to students needs and using learning rate over time and the level of performance to make important educational decisions to guide instruction " (National Reading Panel, 2000).

Typically, Response to Intervention is considered a three tier model. However, some school districts and some states, such as the state of Georgia, employ a four tier model (Bender & Shores, 2007). Whereas, tier four is not commonly referenced in most of the literature on Response to Intervention, this book will operate on the premise of a three-tier model.

For the sake of clarification, let's review the three-tier model:

Tier One of RTI requires consistent high quality classroom instruction which incorporates three nonnegotiable components:

1. ***A standards-based core curriculum***

2. ***Differentiating instruction so that all students can learn***

3. ***A variety of authentic assessments geared to monitoring student progress and driving instruction.***

Tier One

Tier One of RTI requires the use of best practice, research-based teaching methods. Research- based strategies, as discussed in Robert Marzano's *Dimensions of Learning*, are implemented in the differentiated classroom to provide the best teaching practices for Tier One, thereby reducing the need for interventions.

Given my experience teaching at the high school level as both a special education teacher and a co-teacher who worked within the inclusion model, as well as my experience coaching in elementary, middle and high schools around the country, I have become convinced that every classroom needs to begin at Tier One: differentiating instruction so that all students can learn. When teachers differentiate instruction, 80-90% of students are successful in meeting achievement benchmarks. (Hanson, 2009)

1. The verbal linguistic, auditory delivery of information where students are expected to passively sit in their seats and take in information while trying to copy notes at rapid speed does not work for all students.

2. The students it does not work for are the students who are not responding to education and are doing poorly in the classroom as well as on their state tests. While this method may work for some teachers and some students, it does not work for the majority of our struggling student population.

3. A consequence of the lack of differentiation at the classroom level is a. Students that can be successful when shown 'another' way to learn will fail if forced to learn in the same time, in the same way, using the same materials as verbal linguistic learners. b. That students who move on to college, whether to engineering coursework or technical school, primarily learned only one mode of studying. When they become college students and are met with challenging coursework, they often lack the study skills to support them in the more rigorous academic environment. This is why we often find that our most successful high school students don't meet expectations at the college level.

The reality is that until we differentiate instruction at the classroom level, a basic requirement of Tier One RTI, we are shortchanging all our students: English-language learners, students with special needs, trade bound students, or students heading off to college.

Reflection Notes

How do we differentiate instruction?

1. By using teaching strategies that support all intelligence styles and modes of learning, as well as challenging ourselves to implement center activities such as Fitzell Acceleration Centers™, station teaching, and flexible grouping within our pedagogy.
2. Rather than try to cover it all, teachers need to look critically at their standards-based core curriculum and focus on what's most important, thereby allowing time for meaningful teaching, repetition, and student practice.
3. Incorporate multiple modes of assessment. RTI requires authentic assessments; a variety of measures that clearly identify what the student knows and what a student doesn't know.

Again, the most important concept to take away in this chapter is that Response to Intervention is simply "really good teaching."

There are times when students will fail to learn despite the best efforts of the teacher. Master teachers who differentiate instruction and respond to student needs still encounter students who struggle to learn the content required for the curriculum. As teachers take note of the student who is failing to respond to the teaching methodology, they need to consider how to intervene so that students will become successful.

Tier Two

Using curriculum-based measurement practices, teachers determine where the student is lacking and then seek Tier Two interventions that might be appropriate for that student. Often, Tier Two interventions can be researched-based practices used in Tier One, but with three modifications.

1. Specific students receive more intense instruction and application of the strategies.
2. Students are given more time to practice and implement the strategies.
3. The intensity of implementation may increase.

It may be appropriate, at times, to provide Tier Two interventions in a flexible grouping situation in the general classroom. This may prevent students from being pulled out of the classroom, which would cause them to miss critical instruction (Wright, 2007).

If teachers routinely implemented small group work, flexible grouping, or center teaching, then interventions in Tier Two would fall right into place in the lesson plan.

Challenges to implement Tier Two: Having adequate time to implement interventions is often the greatest challenge faced by schools at all grade levels, especially secondary.

1. "Double Dose" Class
2. After school support
3. Tutored study hall

An option that can work quite well is for students to have a tutored intervention session available to them. This is not a resource room, nor a special education resource; rather it is an intervention session where content area teachers, specialists, or support staff are available to implement interventions. This class can be built into the students' day just as a study hall would be at the secondary level.

Providing students with a double dose of the intervention strategies increases the possibility that they ultimately will be successful (Shores & Chester, 2009).

Tier Three

Tier Three is not as delineated as Tier One and Two in literature on Response to Intervention. School districts define Tier Three requirements in a few different ways:

1. More intensive interventions that are based on problem-solving models implemented through a combination of means including classroom instruction, outside of school instruction, or in-school instruction outside of the general classroom.
2. A combination of intensive interventions implemented in general education as well as including special education services.
3. Special education in some school districts is considered Tier Three.

For the purposes of clarity in this book Tier Three is considered a general education process that is implemented before students may be referred for special education services. Once a student is identified as special needs, that student is no longer considered part of the Response to Intervention protocol.

> *"In most schools, Tier Three is not special education but is more intensive intervention to try to improve the progress and avoid the necessity of placement in special education."(Hall, 2008)*

Reflection Notes

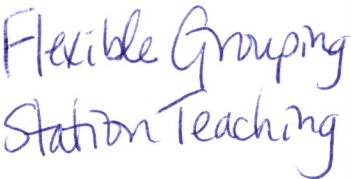

Flexible Grouping –
Station Teaching

Tier Three is the most intensive phase of the RTI three-tier system. At Tier Three, students receive intervention instruction for a longer period of time, with more:

1. Frequency
2. Intensity
3. Time

Students who have not responded to Tier One or Tier Two efforts and who have significant difficulty being successful in the general curriculum might receive:

1. One-to-one
2. One-to-two
3. Or small group intensive instruction

At the elementary level, Tier Three typically incorporates two 30 minute intervention periods every day. This schedule is logistically challenging if not impossible at the middle school and high school level. Intervention teams need to think outside the box in order to come up with realistic intervention schedules.

The general classroom teacher will rarely have time to implement Tier Three interventions. Rather, the general education teacher may choose to use intervention strategies in their lesson plans in tandem with the following:

- Intervention strategies are implemented by specialists, tutors, support staff
- Instructional labs/intervention sessions set up as part of the school schedule.
- Often, intervention schedules at the secondary level for Tier Two and Three must be General Education Versus Special Education and Responsible Inclusion

You may be questioning whether students who need Tier Three interventions, and in some cases Tier Two interventions, should be in the general classroom as opposed to receiving special education services. Because some districts and authors are calling Tier Three "special education," there are two schools of thought. After co-teaching in inclusive classrooms and witnessing the benefits of inclusion done well in schools and school districts around the country, I am convinced that most students achieve more in the general classroom with an environment of excellent teaching.

A small percentage of students are best served within the framework of special education and special classrooms. However, the reality is that this is a small group. In many school districts, special education caseloads are overwhelming. If we properly implement RTI, we allow special education teachers to work more intensely with the students who have the greatest needs.

Response to Intervention provides general educators with the tools to reach most learners while allowing special educators to more effectively meet the needs of the student with special needs.

Reflection Notes

With a system for Response to Intervention in place, teachers can provide instruction that reaches a variety of learning styles, gives additional time where necessary, and monitors progress. The classroom teacher adjusts interventions based on student performance, as determined by progress monitoring. With RTI, classroom teaching is data driven and differentiated

RTI calls upon teachers to break away from the traditional mode of verbal linguistic and auditory teaching, especially at the middle and high school levels. It embraces differentiated instruction that responds to varying student learning styles. Teachers will get the satisfaction of seeing students become more successful than they ever imagined because they intervened with student-centered strategies.

Assessment? Well, I Quiz Every Friday…

How we assess students to determine their understanding of the content that we are teaching is critical to the Response to Intervention process. Schools are becoming more and more locked in to using

- Summative assessment
- Standardized measures of student achievement
- Multiple-choice tests
- And other traditional forms of written assessment

Although one could make an argument that this must be the measure that teachers use because it is the measure required for state testing, it is truly an inaccurate and I would argue unethical, means of evaluating students.

The only true evaluation is authentic assessment. Authentic assessments incorporate a variety of measures into the evaluation process and focuses on formative assessment. Some types of authentic assessment include:

1. Rubrics
2. Exit cards
3. Curriculum-based measurement
4. Student self-evaluation
5. Documented observations

When assessing with a variety of measures, teachers build a portfolio of data that provides a more accurate picture of the student as a learner. With this authentic, data-driven student portrait, teachers have the necessary information to do the problem-solving and detective work required for determining appropriate interventions.

Use assessment for three different purposes. In RTI, three types of assessments are used:

1. Universal screening to determine which students need closer monitoring, differentiated instruction or a specific intervention (3+times/year);
   a) AIMSweb through grade 8
   b) EdCheckup through grade 8
   c) STEEP - isteep.com/datatools.html -- through grade 12
   d) Thinkgate.net (a framework for setting up assessments)
   e) Alternate screening tools
      i) Attendance records
      ii) Grades – failing core academics (especially freshman)
      iii) Student absences: Missed 10 of the first 30 days of school
      iv) Identify students who are over-age for their grade level.
   f) State standardized assessments
2. Progress monitoring to determine if interventions are producing the desired results.
3. Diagnostics to determine what students can and cannot do in important academic areas.

Progress Monitoring versus What We Have Done Historically

Traditional Assessments	Progress Monitoring
• Typically lengthy & time consuming • Administered infrequently or at the end of a unit • Typically students do not receive immediate feedback • Feedback may not inform instructional planning	• Easy and quick method for gathering student performance data • Administered frequently • Students & teachers receive immediate feedback to adjust instruction • Students are compared to peers and local norms

Curriculum Based Measurement (CBM)

Curriculum-based measurement is one form of a scientifically based method for monitoring progress. CBMs describe academic competence, track academic development, and improve student achievement. The three purposes of CBMs are screening, progress monitoring, and instructional diagnosis.

Rubrics

Rubrics are performance-based assessment tools used to evaluate student performance on a task, a set of tasks, or a learning outcome. Rubrics use specific criteria, in the form of narrative descriptions, as a basis for evaluating student performance. Most rubrics use a tabular format that identifies the level of student achievement, from low-to-high or high-to-low, based upon the proficiency that the student is able to achieve. Rating scales may be numerical, qualitative, or both.

The sample lesson plans in this text employ rubrics in order to clearly illustrate performance goals and assist in identifying the level of intervention necessary for different students with each activity. They are also a valid example of a progress-monitoring tool.

Exit cards

Exit cards are a simple assessment tool. Each card will have a set of just two or three questions for students to answer after you teach a lesson. Students answer the questions before the bell rings. It is the last thing they do in class. They must hand the card to the teacher before they walk out the door, hence the name *exit cards*. It's ongoing, immediate assessment in action. Exit cards (a.k.a. *tickets to leave*) are used to gather information on student readiness levels, understanding of concepts just taught, interests, and learning profiles.

Exit cards can be used to form intervention pairs, triads, and groups.

After a lesson, use exit cards to assess student understanding or interest. Keep the items on the cards short and to the point. Keep it simple!

When reviewing the cards that are implemented as an assessment tool, score them with a #1 if the student does not understand the concept, got the answer wrong, or needs re-teaching. Score them with a #2 if the student understands but needs more practice. Score them with a #3 if the student understands the concept and is ready to move on. (Figure 1)

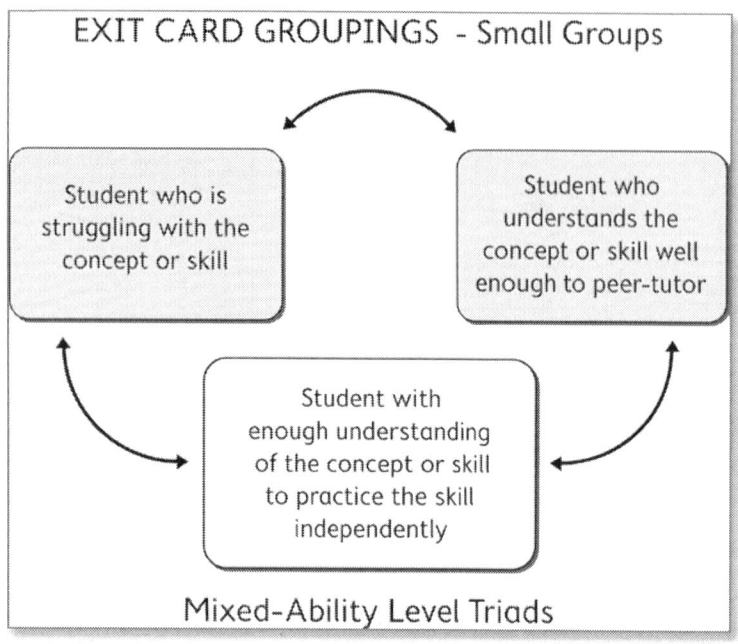

Figure 1: Exit Card Grouping: Mixed Ability Level Triads

Then use the cards to group students.

You might put all the students who received a 1 together and re-teach that group (or small groups). Put those who received a 2 together (or in small groups) and give them a practice activity. Put those who got a 3 together and assign them an enrichment activity, or an investigation.

Alternatively, you might put a 1, a 2, and a 3 together in a triad to practice the skill. (Figure 2)

Additional quick assessments might include:

- High-fluency phrases from *The Fluent Reader* by Timothy V. Rasinski (Raskinski, 2003). Do an Internet search on a paper titled, "Phrases and Short Sentences for Repeated Reading Practice."

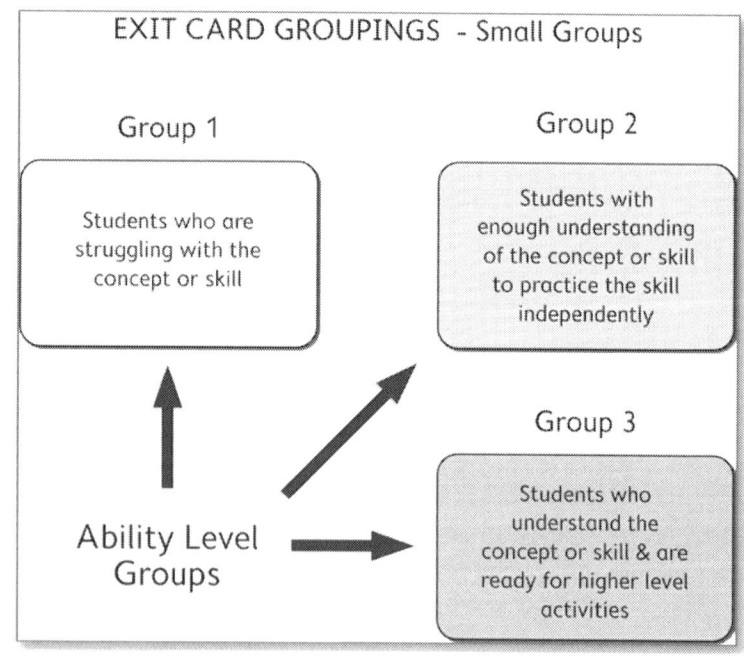

Figure 2: Exit Card Grouping: Ability Level Groups

- Every-Day Edits are also effective as both an assessment and an intervention. Search for Every-Day Edits at

http://www.educationalworld.com

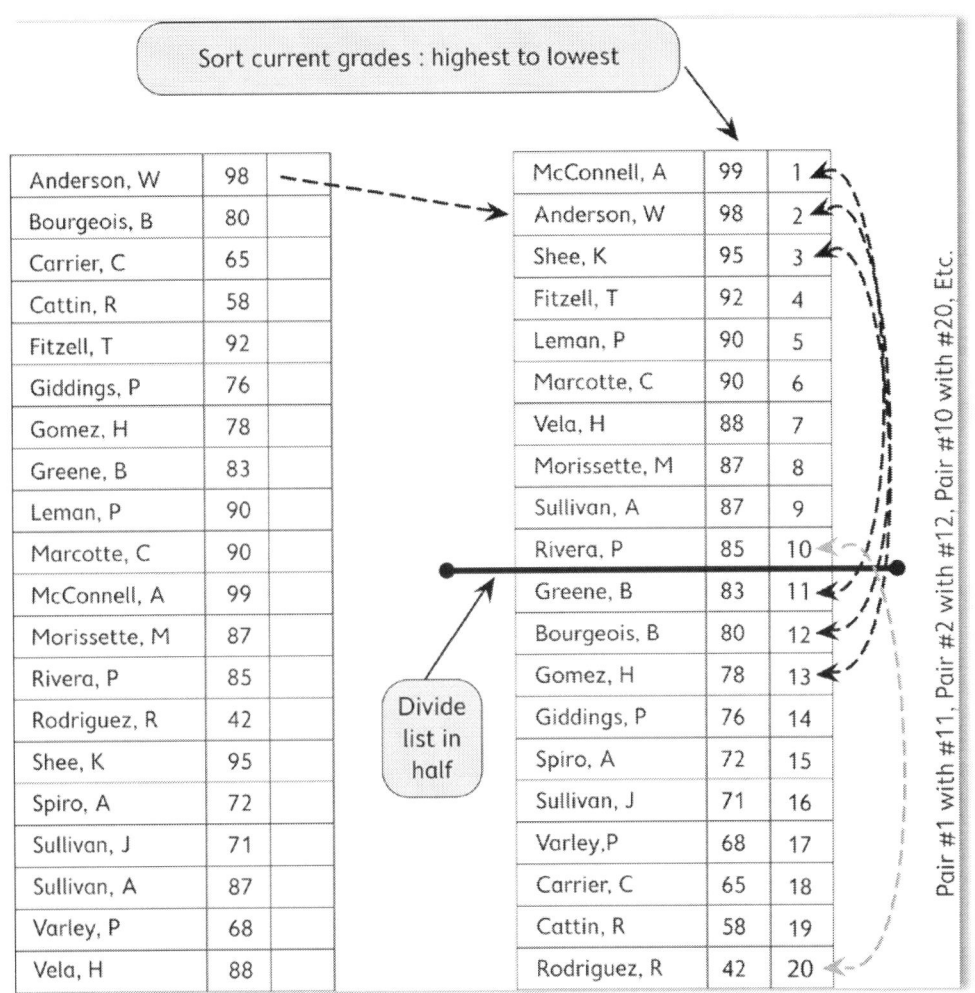

Figure 3: High Middle/Middle Low Grouping Example

Research Based Strategies Incorporated in this Book

The requirement to solely use research-based techniques for interventions initially had me in a fury. Having spent years teaching and working directly with students, whether one-to-one or inclusive classrooms, I firmly believe that there are successful strategies that I use with students that do not have a research study to back them up. Consequently, when told that Response to Intervention required the use of research-based strategies I did some research on 'acceptable research' and in doing so discovered 'single subject experimental design'.

Single subject experimental design is the solution that alleviated my angst. I could use a strategy that I knew worked for many of the students that I've taught over the years as long as I collected data and used the protocol for single subject experimental design. (Brown-Chidsey & Steege, 2005)

Part 2: Chapter 1:
Vocabulary Interventions

Bright Ideas

Use Vocabulary Mapping to Acquire New Vocabulary

Background:

Moore, D. W., & Readence, J. E. suggests that gains in vocabulary knowledge following graphic organizer use may be even greater than gains in comprehension. The average effect size for the 23 studies reviewed was more than twice as large as that reported for comprehension. Thus, graphic organizers appear to be a very effective tool for improving vocabulary knowledge. (Moore, 1984)

Learning Objectives:

1. Acquire new vocabulary
2. Connect that vocabulary to themes and categories
3. Use appropriate questioning to gather information.

Application to Response to Intervention Tiers:

TIER ONE	TIER TWO	TIER THREE
Teacher uses strategy with entire class to differentiate instruction	Student(s) use a structured approach for studying vocabulary using graphic organizers. Student works with a peer tutor, specialist or in a coaching session with the classroom teacher at least twice per week until the study strategy is internalized.	Student works with a specialist one-to-one for an additional 60 to 90 minutes per week using this intervention as a strategy to facilitate reading recall, comprehension and analysis.

Addresses the following non-responder indicators:

- Auditory learning deficit
- Attention Deficit Disorder
- Difficulty connecting new information with previously learned knowledge
- Difficulty linking prior knowledge with new information
- Struggle to effectively use words to express organized and complete thoughts in writing
- Word usage skills below standard
- Difficulty recoding incoming information into meaningful information

Reflection Notes

Materials Needed:

1. Markers
2. Paper
3. Ruler (Optional)

Approximate time frame for completion:

15 minutes

Extension Learning:

Time is variable

Intervention procedure & scripts

Explain to students that vocabulary words are worth points depending on the number of syllables in the word.

Each syllable is worth one point.

Examples:

- Great = 1 point
- Immense = 2 points
- Enormous = 3 points
- And so on...

The groups that have words in their circle that add up to:

- 30 points = C
- 40 points = B
- 60 points = A

They may use a thesaurus.

Tier One/ Whole Group

1. Draw a large circle on the board and write the theme topic in the center of the circle.
2. Have students brainstorm a list of words that come to mind for that theme.
3. One student records the words in the circle.

Assign students to pairs: Use High with middle, middle with Low method of choosing pairs.

1. Explain to the students that they are going to work with a partner to each become an expert on one of the words.
2. Give each student a vocabulary word map (**Error! Reference source not found.**) and draw one on the board. Choose a word from the board and complete a vocabulary word map with the class to demonstrate how to complete one properly.

Tier One/Whole Group

1. Have one person from each group share their word-map with the class and then post their word map on the board. This way the students can use them during their writing if they need help with a word.

Tier Two/Small Group (May also be used at Tier One)

1. Put students in groups of 2 or 3, leveled appropriately.
2. Each group will need a thesaurus and a dictionary.
3. Assign each group one word from the lists the class brainstormed. (You might assign words appropriate to the pair/group's ability level.)
4. Students will work together to complete their word maps. Each person in the group will complete a word map.

Tier Three/One-on-One

Students work with a specialist or one-on-one with the teacher to master the skill.

To Differentiate:
- Differentiate by readiness and Interest
- Include technology tools such as Inspiration Software, FreeMind, Compendium

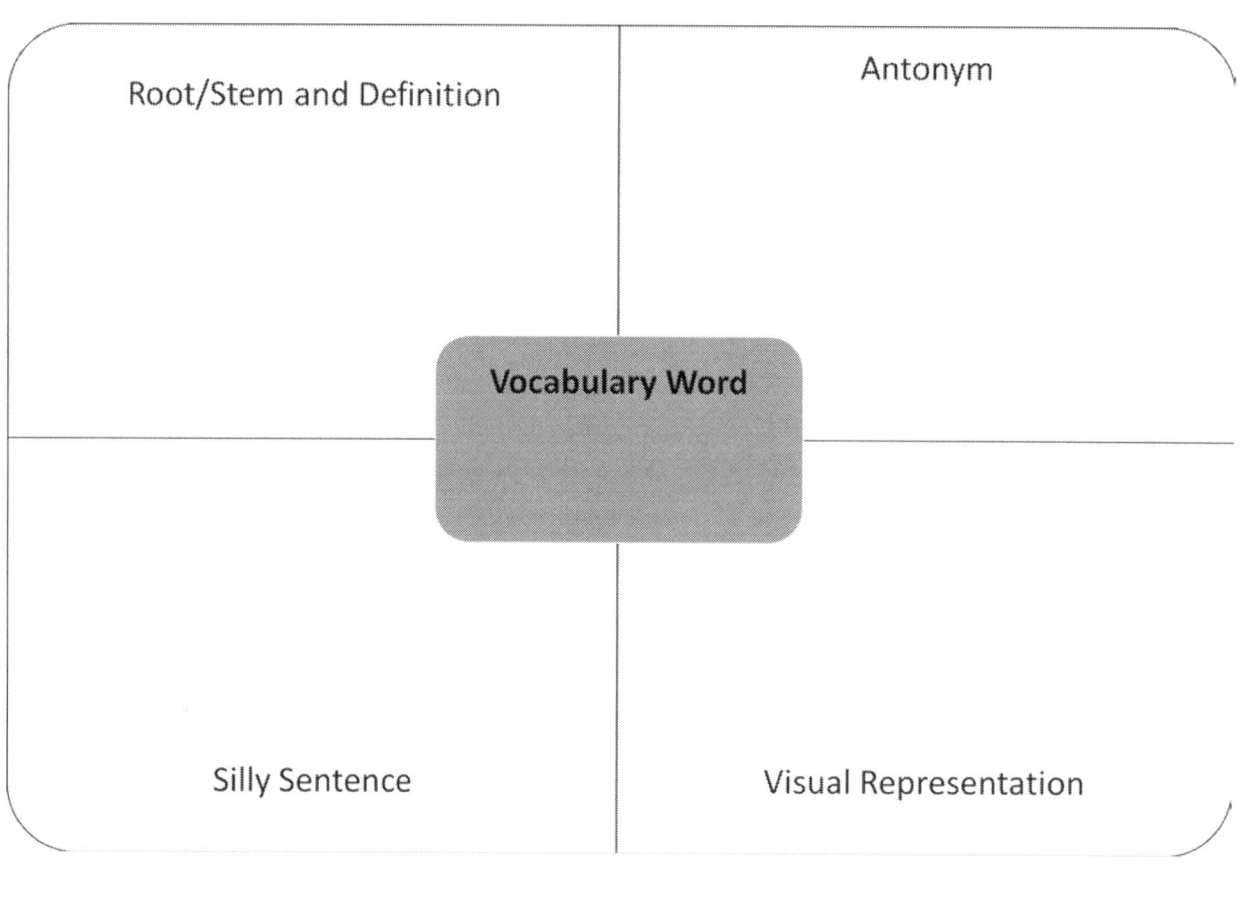

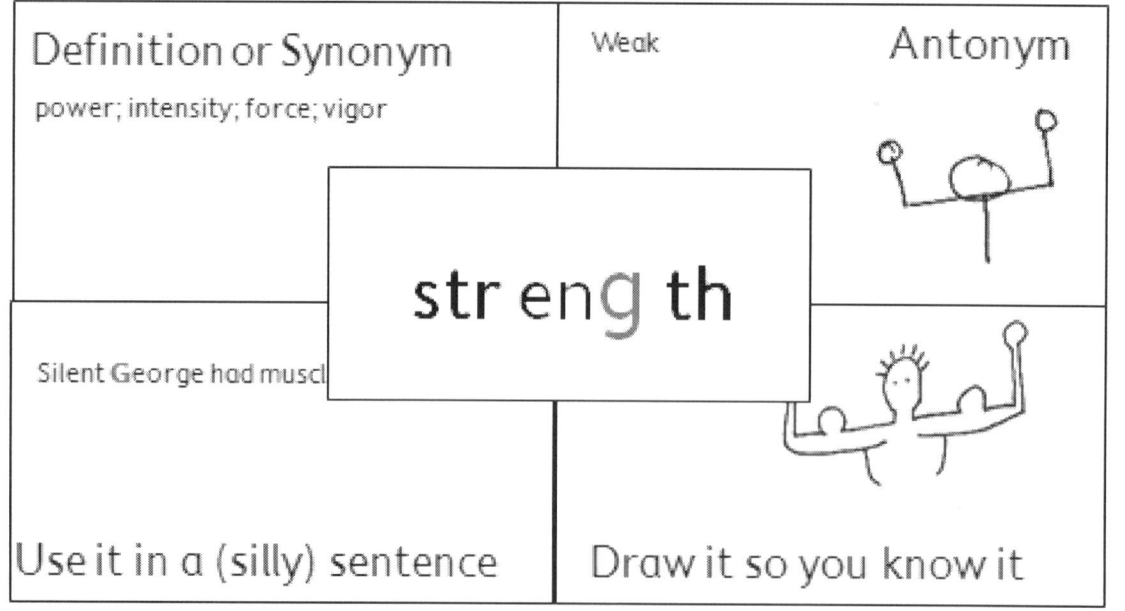

Assessment:

Rubric: Creating Vocabulary Word Maps and Follow-on Assessment

CATEGORY	1	2	3	4
Practice	Made no attempt at completing the vocabulary word map.	Correctly completed 3 steps.	Correctly completed 4 steps.	Correctly completed all 5 steps. 1. Wrote word in center box. 2. Recorded synonyms or a definition. 3. Recorded antonyms. 4. Created an original sentence using the word. 5. Drew a picture representing the word.
Gives enough details and/or creativity in sentence	Sentences less than 4 words lack details or creativity.	Uses an adjective.	Uses an adjective and an adverb.	Uses adjectives, adverbs and or metaphors to create memory cue.
Gives enough details in picture	Almost no details or creativity.	Some details or creativity.	Imagery is creative and shows thought.	Very creative and shows thought behind imagery.
Acquisition (Vocabulary Assessment)	Scored below 70%.	Scored 70% or above.	Scored 80% or above.	Scored 90% or above.

Across the Curriculum:

Whether in Social Studies, Science, or Math teachers can use this approach to have their students use vocabulary word maps to introduce vocabulary related to new themes and to show connections within themes.

Additional Non-Linguistic Interventions:

Many of the students in your class are Bodily-Kinesthetic learners. They learn through their bodies and they need to move. They wiggle and squirm. The following ideas can help make movement be a positive learning force in your classroom.[1]

1. Have your students act out vocabulary words with their bodies. This will give them a visual picture to remember their words.
2. Have the class clap out the syllables in the names of their classmates or their vocabulary words. This is a great strategy for helping kids remember long and multisyllabic words.
3. Kinesthetic Alphabetizing: Put vocabulary words on individual cards and pass them out to the class. Then have them move around the room and, at a signal from you, form groups (of five or less, depending on grade level and vocabulary) and line up in alphabetical order.
4. Kinesthetic Prepositions: Have students use an object such as a pencil and hold it in, under, over, next to, beside, or above their desk to act out prepositions.
5. Have students finger spell their vocabulary and spelling words(Koehler, 1986). [2]
6. Form pictures to connect to vocabulary for visual vocabulary review cards, try www.makebeliefscomix.com – This site is a wonderful tool for teachers and students alike!
7. Building vocabulary skills at home: Suggest to parents that they turn on the closed captioning on TV.

Reflection Notes

---

[1] 1-4 contributed by Fritz Bell author of *Total Body Learning: Movement and Academics.*
[2] Koehler, Linda J. S.; Lloyd, Lyle L., *Using Fingerspelling/Manual Signs to Facilitate Reading and Spelling*, 1986.

Combining Verbal Linguistic and Non-Linguistic:
Practice Strategies for Tier One, Two and Three:

I'm always looking for ways to make learning motivating and fun. Vocabulary development and even spelling are a passion of mine that has been building for the past year. I constantly hear teachers lament that students do not remember vocabulary. Reading deficiencies, many times exacerbated by poor vocabulary development are impacting test scores – both state and SAT and ACT. In addition to that, students are developing their own vocabulary and re-spellings because of text messaging. Those new spellings are making their way into student class work.

So, how about a homework assignment (students may need access to a school computer) that requires students to create a word collage of sorts with a website like http://www.wordle.net/. See **Figure 4 Wordle.net**

Would that encourage practice? It doesn't necessarily assist with the definitions; however, it is possible to include both the word and the definition in the Wordle design. Not only would this be fun, it would be interactive, verbal linguistic AND non-linguistic representation. We have the best of a few worlds of practice with this activity. I'd love to hear others thoughts on this idea.

Wordle.net is also a tool for students to check word overuse in a paragraph or essay. The most used words turn out the largest in the design. If the word nice is overused, it will be larger than all the other words.

Figure 4 Wordle.net

Part 2 Chapter 2:
RTI Strategies for Reading Comprehension

Bright Ideas

Reading Comprehension Intervention: Reciprocal Teaching

Cooperative Learning

Background:

Reciprocal teaching (Lederer, 2000)is an instructional strategy involving discussion as well as using reading strategies (summarizing, question generating, clarifying, and predicting) to improve comprehension of text. Studies by (Palinscar and Brown 1985)(Palincsar, 2002) have proven that reciprocal teaching greatly influences student comprehension skills. They also found that students became readers that are more independent, better summarizers, predictors, and critical thinkers. As an additional benefit, they found that students who participated in reciprocal teaching groups displayed fewer behavior problems. (Lederer, 2000) also stated, "Reciprocal teaching, when used consistently, can produce rapid results and growth in comprehension for readers of all ages."

This lesson plan focuses on using reciprocal teaching to practice a questioning strategy. According to Lubliner (2001), students "automatically increase their reading comprehension when they read the text, process the meaning, make inferences, and connections to prior knowledge, and finally, generate a question."

Learning objectives:

- Identify the different types of questions.
- Formulate different types of questions.
- Work in cooperative groups to practice reading comprehension strategies.
- Synthesize information in order to respond to a variety of questions.
- Interpret text and demonstrate higher level thinking skills in creating various types of questions.
- Enhance comprehension through questioning.
- Apply questioning strategies in many curricular areas.

Application to Response to Intervention Tiers:

TIER ONE	TIER TWO	TIER THREE
Teacher uses strategy with entire class to differentiate instruction	Students work in a small group or dyad with teacher/specialist to Role-play: Interviewing for QARs as a skill building intervention. See the following Tier Two activities	Instead of the Teacher-Student Role-play, the activity is implemented with a student and classroom teacher, specialist or paraprofessional skilled in the QAR method. Student works with a specialist one-to-one for an additional 60-90 minutes per week using this intervention.

Addresses the following non-responder indicators:
- Attention Deficit Disorder
- Reading Difficulties
- Processing Disorders
- Gifted Students
- Difficulty linking prior knowledge to new information
- Difficulty processing information in a way that is meaningful to them.
- Difficulty organizing information
- Difficulty retaining information
- Difficulty finding text support
- Reading fluency
- Reading Difficulties
- Difficulty finding text support
- Difficulty determining what is important in a text
- Self-questioning techniques non-existent or not skilled enough to support understanding while reading.
- accuracy and pace of performance requires extensive effort in order to support reading
- gaps in instruction

Materials Needed:

Literature (magazine or newspaper articles, textbooks, poetry, novels, short stories, non-fiction and fiction texts, websites, blogs)

Approximate time frame for completion:

1. Whole group strategy Introduction and Practice – 30-40 minutes
2. Whole Group/Small Group Practice – 15-20 minutes (variable depending on article length and student participation)
3. Partner Work – 20-30 minutes (variable depending on article length and student understanding)
4. Independent Practice/Peer Feedback – 20-30 minutes (variable depending on article length and student understanding)

Intervention Procedure & Scripts

Tier One: Whole Group

Activity#1

The key to teaching students how to use a particular reading strategy is modeling. Through "think alouds," teachers can demonstrate how to ask questions throughout a reading. (James, 2007)

Reflection Notes

1. Teach students the Question Answer Relationship (QAR) strategy (Raphael 1986). According to the QAR strategy there are two kinds of questions:
   1) Questions in the book
   2) Questions in my head
     a. There are two types of "In the Book" questions:
       i. "Right There" questions are clearly answered in the text.
       ii. "Think and Search" questions are answered within the text but the reader has to search for the answer and synthesize material to find it.
     b. There are two types of "In my Head" questions:
       i. "On My Own" questions can be answered by the reader by synthesizing prior knowledge.
       ii. "Author and Me" questions are those in which the answer is inferred within the text. The reader must use a combination of textual information and prior knowledge to answer the question.
2. Choose a book or article to use to model the questioning strategy.
     a. Read the literature aloud and model your thinking. ("I wonder why the author included this."; "What is a

_____?"; "How would I feel if this happened to me?" etc.).
   b. Read another book or article with the class.
   c. Create a **questioning web(See Figure 5 Questioning Web)** on chart paper to incorporate all of the students' questions.
3. Go over the **questioning web** and discuss what type of questions, according to the QAR method, each one exemplifies.

Tier One/Tier Two - Whole Group/Small Group

Role-play: Interviewing for QARs

This interviewing activity can be done either with the whole class or in smaller groups.

1. After reading specified material, choose one to five students to be the "interviewee(s)". These students can take on the role of a character in the reading, an historical figure, or a scientist (whatever suits your purpose).
2. The rest of the class represents "the interviewers." Each student is to come up with at least four questions to ask the interviewee(s). Challenge them to ask one question from each QAR category. (They can do this in pairs if it is difficult for them.)
3. Have students take turns asking questions and eliciting responses from the interviewees. Interviewers should try to ask all different types of questions. Interviewees should try to "be their character" and use information from the reading to guide their responses.
4. Wrap-up the discussion. Have students give examples of questions that classmates asked to demonstrate each QAR classification.

Tier One/Tier Two - Partner Work

Role-play: Teacher and Student

In this intervention activity, students will practice being the "teacher" and the "student." The "teacher" will ask the "student" questions. This strategy not only emphasizes questioning ("teacher"), but also reinforces other comprehension strategies ("student" and "teacher") including summarizing, synthesizing, etc. depending on the types of questions the "teacher" creates.

1. Divide students into pairs.
2. Provide them with their reading materials (pages in a textbook, a literature chapter, an article, etc.) and have them read the material together.
3. As students read they should fill out individual question webs.
4. Appoint one student in each dyad the role of "teacher" and the other the role of "student".
5. The "teacher" asks the "student" questions. The "student" responds to the question using the text for support. When they are finished, they can switch roles. Challenge the "student" to think of questions the "teacher" did not ask.

6. The partners should then evaluate each question. They can tally how many times they used each type of QAR question. If they are having trouble creating certain types of questions, they can go back and work together to create new ones.

Tier Three: Specialist/Teacher and Student

Instead of the Teacher-Student Role-play outlined above, the activity is implemented with a student and classroom teacher, specialist or paraprofessional skilled in the QAR method.

Grouping Suggestions
- Random grouping (counting off, toe-to-toe, etc.)
- Strong reader/struggling reader
- Similar ability levels (adjust material accordingly)

Differentiating Instruction: Support Suggestions

- Provide students with a bookmark(See Figure 6 QAR Bookmarks) or a desk template to help them remember the different types of questions.
- Step One: Have students use a questioning web to brainstorm questions from a text/math problem. Step Two: Sort the questions according to the QAR model. This frees up the students' working memories to create questions without the added step of categorizing. Categorize according to QAR later.
- Mixed Ability QAR: Students can work in groups to create questions. Assign students who are experiencing the most difficulty formulating questions the "Right There" questions and the most advanced students the "Author and Me" questions.

Application Examples:
Your class just finished reading the first chapter of _The Story of My Life_ by Helen Keller.
1. Assign each student a partner.
2. Each pair develops a question web together.
3. Students then work together to classify each question into one of the QAR categories.
4. Choose four students to be the "interviewees." They will represent Helen's mother, Helen's brother, Helen's father and Helen.
5. The rest of the class will take turns addressing questions to each character.
6. Make a giant chart and have the class give examples of each type of question asked.
7. Discuss what types of questions students find easier/harder to compose and answer. Have students offer suggestions to classmates as to how to overcome obstacles.

Across the Curriculum:
This strategy can be applied to many curricular areas. For example:

- **Social Studies and Science:** Students can read using the QAR strategy to guide questions for a research project.
- **Tests:** Students can use the QAR strategy to help them study for a test in any course.

- **Math:** The QAR framework supports comprehension of word problems especially in relations to graphs or tables displaying data.

For independent writing assignments:
Students can use the questioning strategy for independent writing assignments by using their questions to instigate research projects, journal, or essay writing.

For independent reading assignments (literature or content area):
Students can use the questioning strategy as a tool to check for understanding.

For group brainstorming and mind map creation:
The questioning strategy is ideal for cooperative learning. Students can challenge one another, help one another understand material, and develop discussions through questioning.

Extension:
Students may select their own articles in order to find material that meets their interest and academic ability level. They can create quizzes for one another. They can pose questions that lend to further research and investigation.

QAR Authentic Assessment Activity

1. Have students practice the QAR approach independently.
2. Read a piece of literature and write down their questions using a question web as they read.
3. Have them use the QAR graphic organizer (See Figure 7 QAR Graphic Organizer) to help categorize each of their questions.
4. Go back and add more questions to any categories that need more. Students should try to answer their own questions.
5. Exchange papers with a partner. Answer the questions AND provide feedback on the quality of questions.

Assessment:

Rubric: Summarizing Pieces of Literature

CATEGORY	1	2	3	4
In the Book: "Right There" Questions & "Think and Search" Questions	Does not identify or create "In the Book" questions accurately.	Does not consistently identify or create "In the Book" questions.	Accurately identifies and creates "In the Book" questions.	Identifies and creates "In the Book" questions appropriately linked to the text, reflecting close, careful reading.
In My Head: "On My Own" Questions & "Author and Me" questions.	Does not identify or create "In My Head" questions accurately.	Does not consistently identify or create "In My Head" questions.	Accurately identifies and creates "In My Head" questions.	Identifies and creates "In My Head" questions with clarity of thought and higher level thinking skills (demonstrates perceptive reading skills).

Questioning Web:

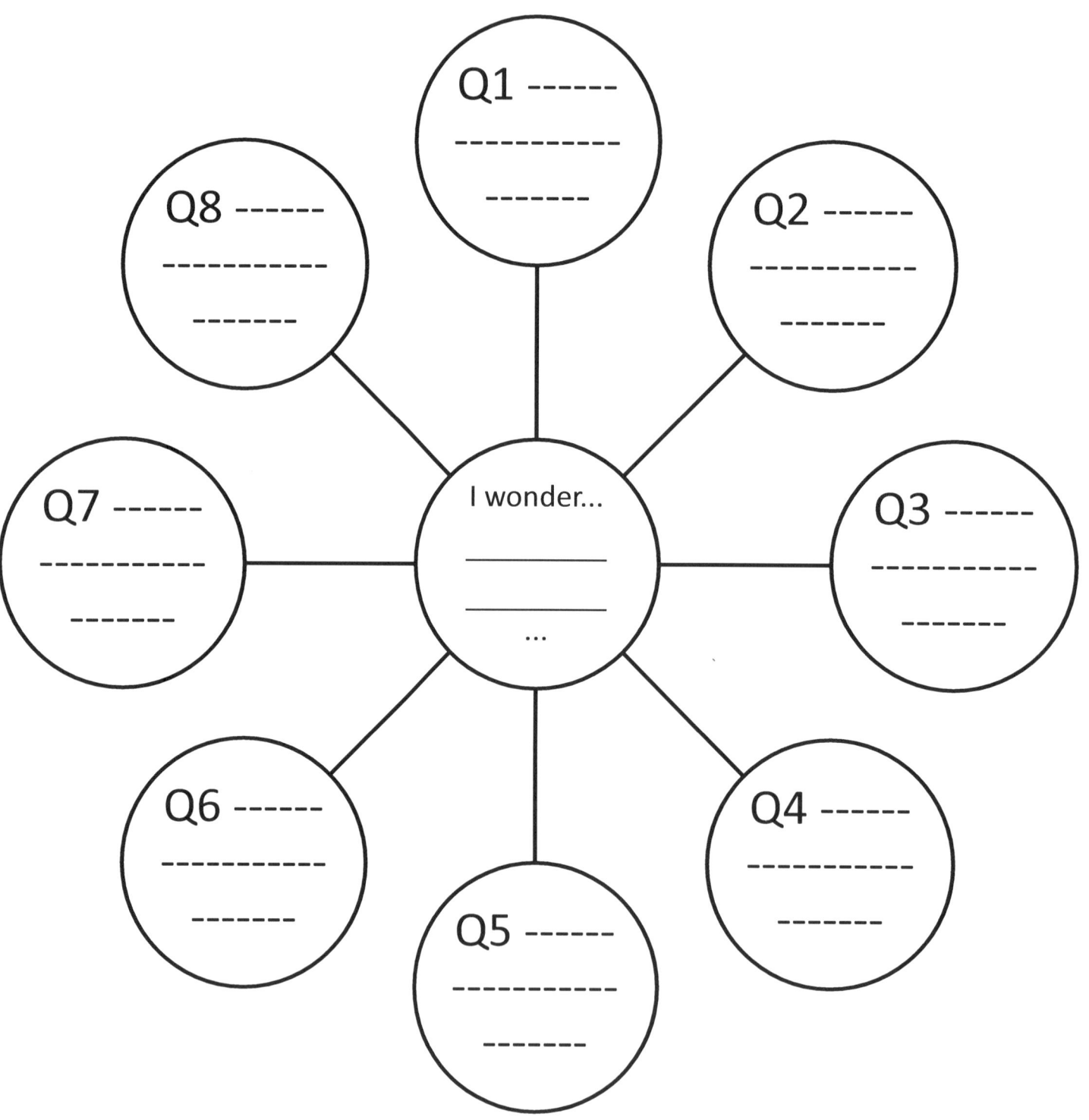

Figure 5 Questioning Web

Questioning Bookmarks:

Types of Questions:

RightThere (The answer is clearly answered in the text.)

Think & Search (The answers are within the text but the reader has to search for it and synthesize material to find it.)

On My Own (Can be answered based on the reader's own experiences and prior knowledge.)

Author & Me (The answer is inferred within the text. The reader must use a combination of textual information and prior knowledge.)

Types of Questions:

RightThere (The answer is clearly answered in the text.)

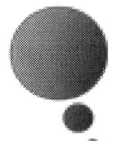

Think & Search (The answers are within the text but the reader has to search for it and synthesize material to find it.)

On My Own (Can be answered based on the reader's own experiences and prior knowledge.)

Author & Me (The answer is inferred within the text. The reader must use a combination of textual information and prior knowledge.)

Types of Questions:

RightThere (The answer is clearly answered in the text.)

Think & Search (The answers are within the text but the reader has to search for it and synthesize material to find it.)

On My Own (Can be answered based on the reader's own experiences and prior knowledge.)

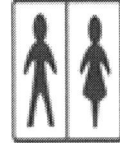

Author & Me (The answer is inferred within the text. The reader must use a combination of textual information and prior knowledge.)

Figure 6 QAR Bookmarks

QAR Graphic Organizer

Right There
(The answer is clearly answered in the text.)

Think and Search
(The answers are within the text but the reader has to search for it and synthesize material to find it.)

On My Own
(Can be answered based on the reader's own experiences and prior knowledge)

Author and Me
(The answer is inferred within the text. The reader must use a combination of textual information and prior knowledge.)

Figure 7 QAR Graphic Organizer

Picture Books: A Reading Intervention for K-12

Research Background

Lower elementary teachers reading this handbook are fully aware of the value of using picture books as a teaching tool. Upper elementary teachers as well as secondary educators may not realize that research indicates that picture books used in the upper grade levels may improve student comprehension as well.

In a study by Bridget Robinson at the University of North Carolina (Robinson, 2007), high school students who studied literary terms with picture books were 72% more successful on a test of literary terms than those who studied using traditional means. Students found it easier to understand and recall literary terms when picture books were used as a teaching tool.

Picture books help students create mental models (Bickmore, 2001) and help readers build schema. They are written at a reading level accessible to most readers, with content varying to meet individual needs. They help students understand complex ideas and vocabulary. Consider that although picture books typically are written for pre-K children, they are meant to be read aloud and therefore utilize high-level vocabulary. We are also finding more and more picture books with adult themes.

The shorter length of picture books permits students to practice their reading strategies and enhance their understanding of difficult content (Fox & Short, 2003). Picture books allow teachers to "bring up issues, problems, and concerns without deluging students with facts and information" (Harvey, 2007, p. 69). Another advantage to the shorter length of picture books is that student reading and response is plausible within the brief class periods educators face in secondary schools (Johnson Nancy J., 2007).

For the ELL student, picture books provide a nonthreatening tool with visual cues to support English language acquisition. In a research study focused on using picture books and literature-based instruction with high school ESL students, Nancy L. Hadaway and JaNae Mundy found that using picture books engaged students in the language learning process. Vocabulary increased, and reading comprehension skills were evident through class discussion and through writing about their reading experience through journaling, poetry, and research presentations (Hadaway & Mundy, 1999).

Learning objectives:

- Use picture books to improve comprehension.
- Identify factual information within picture books.
- Make connections to their self, other texts, and the world.
- Synthesize information and present it in a way that is meaningful to them.

Application to Response to Intervention Tiers:

TIER ONE	TIER TWO	TIER THREE
Teacher uses strategy with entire class to differentiate instruction in a multi-ability classroom.	Student(s) use both fiction and nonfiction picture books to practice comprehension strategies until skills are internalized.	Student works with a specialist one-to-one for an additional 60-90 minutes per week using this intervention until skills are internalized.

Reflection Notes

Addresses the following non-responder indicators:

- Reading fluency
- Reading Difficulties
- Difficulty finding text support
- Difficulty determining what is important in a text
- self-questioning techniques non-existent or not skilled enough to support understanding while reading.
- accuracy and pace of performance requires extensive effort in order to support reading
- gaps in instruction
- Attention Deficit Disorder
- Reading comprehension difficulties
- Processing disorders
- Poor reading fluency
- Difficulty linking prior knowledge to new information
- Difficulty finding text support
- Difficulty determining what is important in a text

Materials Needed:

- Picture books related to the topic being discussed

Useful websites:

http://www.uiowa.edu/~crl/bibliographies/pdf/picbooks_print.pdf

http://picturebooksforolderreaders.pbworks.com/

Approximate time frame for completion:

- Whole Group – 30 minutes (variable depending on discussion)
- Small Group – 20 minutes (variable depending on book length and student participation)
- Independent Practice – 30 minutes (variable depending on book length and student understanding)

Intervention procedure & scripts

Tier One/Whole Group

Picture books can be used as a springboard for a new unit of study. They will capture the students' interest, provide some visual images and background information, and, if you choose a high-quality book, trigger questions and discussions that you can use to guide further instruction.

1. Choose a picture book that meets your instructional purpose.
2. Read the story aloud to the class. (Make sure all students can see the powerful pictures.)
3. Discuss the book. Some guiding questions may be:
   - What did you learn about (the subject) from this story?
   - What questions do you have about this topic?
   - What would you like to know more about?
   - What emotions did this story stir inside of you?
   - What facts did this story provide?
   - What impact did the illustrations have in the story?
   - What are the benefits of using picture books to understand this concept (If your students are skeptical about using picture books)?
   - How did (specific situation) impact (specific character)? How can you relate?

Tier One/Tier Two: Small Group

Take it up a Level: Coding Strategy as an Intervention

The Coding Strategy (Harvey 2007) is a great way to help students practice finding the important information in texts. Many of the picture books they use will be fictional stories used to teach a particular concept. By coding the text they will be able to sort out the relevant information from that which is unnecessary. They will also incorporate reading comprehension strategies while thinking critically about the text. Students should use sticky notes to code their information and can use any code that makes sense to them. Some suggestions may be:

(L) Learned New Fact
(*) Interesting Information
(E) Evoked Emotion
(?) Questions

(T) Thoughts
(C) Connections

1. Place students in mixed ability groups (2-4 per group).
2. Give each group a picture book that illustrates your learning goal.
3. Have the group read one page at a time aloud.
4. After each page, group members should discuss whether they found any places where they might use a sticky note to "code" it.
   On each sticky note, students should not only write the letter code, but also a few words to remind them of their thinking.

> **L: Rosa Parks went to jail.**

> **?: I wonder if Rosa Parks knew Dr. Martin Luther King.**

5. Repeat this process through the entire book or reading excerpt.
6. When students are finished, they should go back and review all of their notes.

Tier Three: One-on–one

Both picture book reading and coding strategy can be used as intensive interventions. The picture book strategy would be an intervention that could eventually be eliminated with skill mastery. The coding strategy could be a learning tool that the student uses all through elementary school and through high school and college.

Optional Suggestions:

- Fact Blast: List all of the facts they learned.
- Research answers to their questions.
- Emotion Reaction: Write a reaction to one of the parts that evoked emotion or thought.
- Summarize their story to the class.
- Personal Connection: Discuss connections to other text, self, and world.

Extension Activities:

- Have students find 10 different picture books on a specific topic and complete a graphic organizer for each book. They will choose the best book to present to the class.
- Have students write their own children's book about a specific topic either fiction or non-fiction.
- Complete a Venn diagram comparing/contrasting a picture book with a text book (or compare/contrast two picture books on the same topic).
- Use a picture books to frame a research project.

Application Example:
Picture books can be used to understand and support a thematic unit. For example, you may be doing a unit on "Tough Times." Each student can choose a different picture book that surrounds this theme. This is such a general theme that students may interpret it as war, poverty, death, etc.

1. Each student chooses a book to support the theme. For instance:
   - *Rose Blanc* by Roberto Innocenti (WWII),
   - *Aunt Harriet's Underground Railroad in the Sky* by Jeanette Winter (Slavery),
   - *Fly Away Home* by Eve Bunting (Homelessness),
   - *My Hiroshima* by Junko Morimoto (Hiroshima Bombing)

   Students read their books and complete a graphic organizer.

2. Hold class discussions or assign writing prompts in which all students relate their book to the overall theme.
   - What situations in your own life can you relate to the situation in your book?
   - How does your book demonstrate "Tough Times"?
   - What lessons did you learn in your book that you can apply to any tough times you may face in your life?
   - What events/details in the story made it seem real to you? What feelings did it evoke?

To Differentiate:
Using picture books allows for infinite options for differentiation.
- Use picture books with no words and have students provide information based on the pictures.
- Vary the use of non-fiction and fiction picture books.
- Challenge students to find primary sources.
- Utilize creative grouping strategies.
- Make assignments as focused or broad as the individual student requires.

Across the Curriculum:
This strategy can be applied to many curricular areas.
In English, picture books can be used to teach literary devices. Here are some ideas:
- Alliteration (Chicken Little by Steven Kellog),

- Metaphor (<u>The Stranger</u> by Chris Van Allsburg)
- Irony (<u>The Frog Prince, Continued</u> by Jon Scieszka)
- Satire (<u>The Happy Hocky Family</u> by Lane Smith)
- Personification (<u>Sylvester and the Magic Pebble</u> by William Steig)
- Symbolism (<u>Tar Beach</u> by Faith Ringold)

In Social Studies, picture books can be used to help students relate to a character, time period, and situation.
- Civil War(<u>Nettie's Trip South</u> by Ann Turner)
- Holocaust (<u>The Butterfly</u> by Patricia Polcco)
- WWII (<u>All Those Secrets of the World</u> By Jane Yolen)

In Science, picture books can be used to help students understand complex scientific principles. Students might create their own illustrations to exemplify a concept or explain a concept in simplified terms as if teaching it to a young child. (<u>Science Verse</u> by Jon Scieszka)

In Math, students can create picture books to break down the steps of solving a higher level mathematical problem. There are also many great picture books that teach mathematical concepts. (The "Sir Cumference" series by Cindy Neuschwander)

Picture books can be used to model writing traits. (<u>An Annotated Bibliography for Use with the 6-Trait Analytic Model of Writing Assessment and Instruction</u> by <u>Spandel and Culham 1994</u>)

For Independent Writing Assignments:
Picture books are excellent resources to guide writing. They teach grammar rules, sentence structure, sentence fluency, word choice, syntax, writing for specific purposes, organization, and creativity among other things. Students can find examples within picture books or create their own books.

For Independent Reading Assignments (literature or content area):
Students can apply coding and comprehension skills to more sophisticated types of literature including novels, textbooks, websites, and poetry.

For Group Brainstorming and Mind Map Creation:
Students can help one another to understand a process or idea through brainstorming and mind mapping. They can work together to locate, read, or create picture books.

Extension:
The use of picture books lends itself to a myriad of extension activities. Many suggestions are listed in the lesson ideas above. One key to motivating students is to provide choice. For

example, they could choose a particular theme and create a bibliography of children's books that pertain to that idea.

Assessment:

Independent Implementation:

Have students practice coding picture books independently.

a) Read a picture book and use sticky notes to code information.
b) Complete a graphic organizer using the noted information.

Rubric: Coding Text to Enhance Comprehension Skills

CATEGORY	1	2	3	4
Facts	Does not distinguish between fact and fiction.	Locates facts but confuses some with fictional information.	Locates most of the factual information in a variety of texts.	Locate concretes and inferential facts in a variety of texts.
Questions	Does not formulate questions from the text.	Asks very literal questions from the text.	Asks many different types of questions.	Shows keen comprehension of the text with general questions relating to the "big picture," inferential questions; often researches for more information.
Connections	Does not relate text to other examples.	Makes loose or limited (text, self, world only) connections.	Makes valid connections.	Connects with other text, self, and the world; relates specific situations to big picture ideas.

Name _____
Date _____

Coding Picture Books

Title _____

Author_____

Subject_____

Why I chose this book _____

_____

What I learned _____

_____

_____

_____

Facts_____

_____

_____

_____

_____

_____

Interesting Information _____

_____

_____

_____

_____

Further Questions _____

_____

_____

_____

_____

Connections (Text, Self, World) _____

_____

Thoughts/Emotions _____

What illustrations stuck out or helped you better understand the concept? Explain.

Does this book help support the subject you're learning about? Why or why not?

Tier One, Two or Three Intervention: Ask Questions

Another effective strategy is to ask questions at the end of a reading. Have a template with questions like:

- Has anything like this ever happened to me?
- Did I ever feel this way? *(The brain remembers what's emotional.)*
- Does this happen in my neighborhood?

At the end of each reading, have students answer a question in their journal or notebook, or answer a question to a partner (for students who might struggle too hard to write an answer). This strategy can also be used for homework. Send a list of questions home with a reading assignment and have students answer the questions with their parents or a sibling.

Storyboards[3] as an Intervention

To make a storyboard, have students fold a piece of paper into squares and draw about what they read. They might do this while they read a story for the first time, as a review with a partner, or for homework after a reading assignment. The process of turning verbal information into a visual format reinforces the learning and helps keep the information in working memory longer.

Intervention for Difficulty Sequencing: Sequencing Strips

To remember information in sequence, such as a timeline in history, a cycle in science, or the chronology of a story, use adding machine tape or strips of paper and have students draw their storyboard in sequence. Now they can see the sequence of the storyline, timeline, or process literally in visual, sequential format.

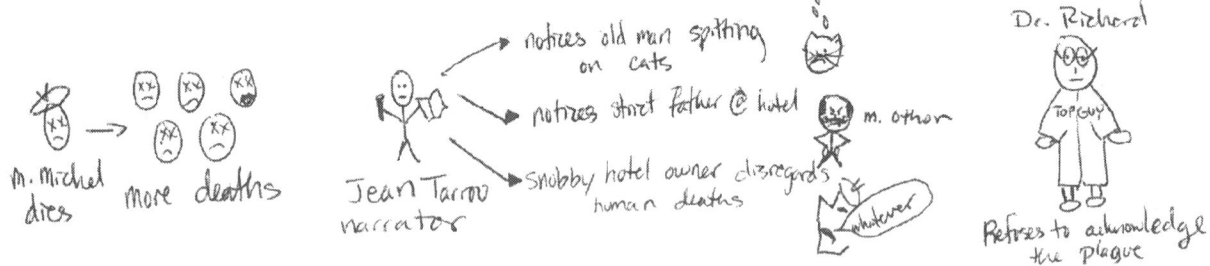

Figure 8 Sequencing Strip High School From Albert Camus' "The Plague"

---

[3] Memorization and Test Taking Strategies for the Differentiated, Inclusive and RTI Classroom by Susan Gingras Fitzell, Cogent Catalyst Publications, 2010

Part 2 Chapter 3:
RTI Strategies for Writing

Bright Ideas

Writing Paragraphs: Grouping & Organizing Information

Friendly Letter to an Author

Background:

The creation of a mind map in a small group is an active and collaborative learning exercise. Because a mind map captures a specific topic in a nonlinear fashion and incorporates graphics and colors, this exercise also can connect with learners whose style is not well served by traditional linear, text-based materials. (Hyerle, 2009; Marzano & Mid-continent Regional Educational Laboratory., 1991; Marzano, Pickering, Pollock, & ebrary Inc., 2001; O'Donnell & King, 1999; Pehrsson & Denner, 1989)

Learning Objectives:

- Organize information according to a theme
- Write a friendly letter in the proper format.
- Support the main idea of a paragraph.
- Use appropriate questioning to find additional information.

Application to Response to Intervention Tiers:

TIER ONE	TIER TWO	TIER THREE
Teacher uses strategy with entire class to differentiate instruction	Student(s) use a structured approach for writing using graphic organizers. Student works with a peer tutor, specialist or in a coaching session with the classroom teacher at least twice per week until the study strategy is internalized.	Student works with a specialist one-to-one for an additional 60 to 90 minutes per week using this intervention as a strategy to facilitate reading recall, comprehension and analysis.

Addresses the following non-responder indicators:

- Note taking deficiencies
- Attention Deficit Disorder
- Difficulty distinguishing the correct from the incorrect written word
- Difficulty organizing information
- Low clerical aptitude – difficulty completing written work
- Difficulty effectively using words to express organized and complete Thoughts in writing
- Below standard word usage skills
- Inability to set writing goals – inattention and regulation problems when writing
- Gaps in instruction

Reflection Notes

Materials needed:

- A selection of books from popular authors
- Rubric
- Friendly letter pieces
- Blank graphic organizers
- Colored pencils or markers
- Note cards

Approximate time frame for completion:

- Main Lesson: Two class periods
- Extension Learning: Variable

Intervention Procedure & Scripts

Tier One /Whole Group

Introduction to Friendly Letter

*The following kinesthetic memory strategy is perfectly appropriate for 6th & 7th graders. Whether a teacher can 'pull it off' in grades 8-12 is dependent on the dynamics of the class and/or the teacher's approach.

Review the parts of a friendly letter with your students using the following movement strategy.
- Stand up and touch their head for the letter heading,
- Wave for the greeting,
- Do a silly pose with their body for the body of a letter.
- Have them pretend to slam a door for the closing

- Then have students sign their name in the air for the signature of the letter.

Tier One/Small Group

1. Place students in preselected small groups (3-5 students) to insure a mixture of ability levels.
2. Hand out a mixed-up pack of different parts of a friendly letter to each group along with the titles for each. There should be enough for each group (Heading, greeting, body (3 paragraphs), closing, and signature).
3. Have each group put their letter together, in order, and attach the appropriate titles. This can be a timed activity if it will be fun for the students and not cause them undue stress.
4. Walk around and monitor students' work.

Time Modification for Tier One/Small Group

Give each group one part of the friendly letter and one title. Have them work with other groups to put them on the board in proper order.

Tier One /Whole Group

1. Explain to the students that they are going to write a letter to their favorite author using the friendly letter format.
2. On the board, brainstorm a list of the students' favorite authors and their books using a web organizer. Write the words "Favorite Authors" in the center. Then write the author's names in one color and the books they have written in another.
3. Hand out the friendly letter graphic organizer and complete each part as a class on the board. Then walk around and assist the students as they complete theirs.

Friendly Letter Template

Heading: Check to make sure you have the correct information on the correct line. It should be on the right side of the paper. See below. You will use the school Address.

> **First line** - street number and street name
> **Second line** - town or city, state and ZIP code
> **Third line** – today's date

Let's Get Started: _____

Street number and Street name
City or Town, State and Zip code
Today's Date

Greeting or Salutation: Dear (Author's first and last name), (remember your comma!)

Introduction: This part is intended to get the author to want to continue reading and to give the author an idea about why you're writing. Tell the author who you are and a little about yourself.

Who are you? _____

What are your hobbies or interests? _____

Body: This is the main part of the letter. Ask the author some questions about the book. Ideas: How did you get the idea for this book? Was the main character designed after someone you know? How long did it take you to write this book? Where do you write?

Paragraph 1: Why I liked this book overall.

Write down a strong lead sentence: For example, I really enjoyed your book, "My Sister's Keeper"

_____

_____

_____

_____

_____

_____

Write down two more things you enjoyed about the book.

_____

_____

_____

Paragraph 2: The character and scenes or events you liked the most.

Write down a strong lead sentence about your favorite character or scene in the book. For example, "Oliver was my favorite because…"

_____

_____

Write two more sentences about your favorite character or scene.

_____

_____

_____

_____

_____

_____

_____

Reflection Notes

Paragraph 3: Questions for the Author

Write down a strong lead sentence: For example, I would like to know some more about how you write your books.

_____

_____

Write down one or two more questions you have for the author. For example, "Where do you do most of your writing",

_____

_____

Explain how you connected to the text or the characters.

_____

_____

Conclusion: Wrap it all up and thank the author for their time.

_____

_____

Closing: Choose an appropriate closing (sincerely, your fan, best regards) and sign your name. Make sure your closing agrees with the heading. Only the first word is capitalized.

_____

Signature: Usually in cursive.

_____

Tier Two/Partner Work:

1. Have students use their graphic organizers **(See Figure 9 Friendly Letter Graphic Organizer)**to write letters to their favorite authors. Remind them that this is the rough draft.
2. Check their drafts against the rubric and edit as necessary.
3. Students then exchange their self-edited letter and rubric with their partner and peer edit.
4. After each pair has edited their work, they schedule conference time with their teacher[4].
5. Students work on final drafts incorporating teacher feedback.

Tier Three:

Follow the instructions above for partner work; however, include the support of a specialist. Allow additional time to practice the skills required to complete the steps. A tier three strategy would include graphic organizers, creating drafts, partner/teacher editing, and final draft _for all writing exercises_ so that the process becomes internalized. Students need to be given adequate time to complete writing activities so that they can move through each step unrushed.

To differentiate:

- Students could work in mixed ability groups
- Offer choices. Allow students to choose the author they wish to write about

Across the curriculum:

- Social Studies teachers can use this approach to have the students write friendly letters to historical characters as if they where a friend who lived in that time.
- Science teachers can use friendly letters to write letters to a favorite scientist, inventor, etc. Or, my personal favorite: Write a letter to a state representative regarding an environmental issue about which the student is passionate.
- Math teachers can use friendly letters to write letters (writing prompts) about math terminology. Their letters simply take what would normally be a short answer response and personalize it. For example, a line graph writes a letter to the Graph family and explains why 'he' is related to the bar graphs and circle graphs in the family.

Extension Activities:

Students might choose one of the following:

- Write an alternate ending to their favorite book
- Write a review of their favorite book, or draw an alternate cover.

For Independent Reading:

Have students read another book by their favorite author and compare and contrast the two.

The students may create a mini-autobiography about their favorite author or pretend they are a reporter and write an interview with their favorite author.

---

[4] If conference time is limited, consider using audio taped feedback.

Assessment:

Friendly Letter Rubric

CATEGORY	1	2	3	4
Neatness and Presentation	Illegible in many places, numerous author and book related words are misspelled. More than one section (heading, greeting, body, closing, signature) is missing or out of order.	Sloppy with several author or book related words misspelled. One or more sections (heading, greeting, body, closing, signature) is missing, out of order, or not in proper format.	Neat and orderly in overall appearance and format.	Margins are present on all four sides and text is visually centered on top and bottom. Spacing follows correct friendly letter format with spaces between paragraphs.
Letter Parts	Has three or less letter parts.	Has four of the five letter parts.	Has date, greeting, body, closing, and signature.	Has heading, greeting, body, closing, and signature.
Conventions	Punctuation, spelling, and grammar significantly distract the reader. There are more than ten errors.	Punctuation, spelling, and grammar slightly distract the reader. There are seven errors or less.	Very good punctuation, spelling, and grammar with less than three errors	Excellent punctuation, spelling, and grammar with less than five errors.
Understanding	An introduction, relevant comments about the author's work or appropriate questions are missing.	Introduction is weak, comments are irrelevant, or the questions are generic.	Letter includes an introduction, relevant comments about the author's work, and asks good questions.	Letter includes specific comments about the author's work and asks excellent questions. Letter is three or more paragraphs. Letter encourages a response from the reader. .

Friendly Letter Graphic Organizer

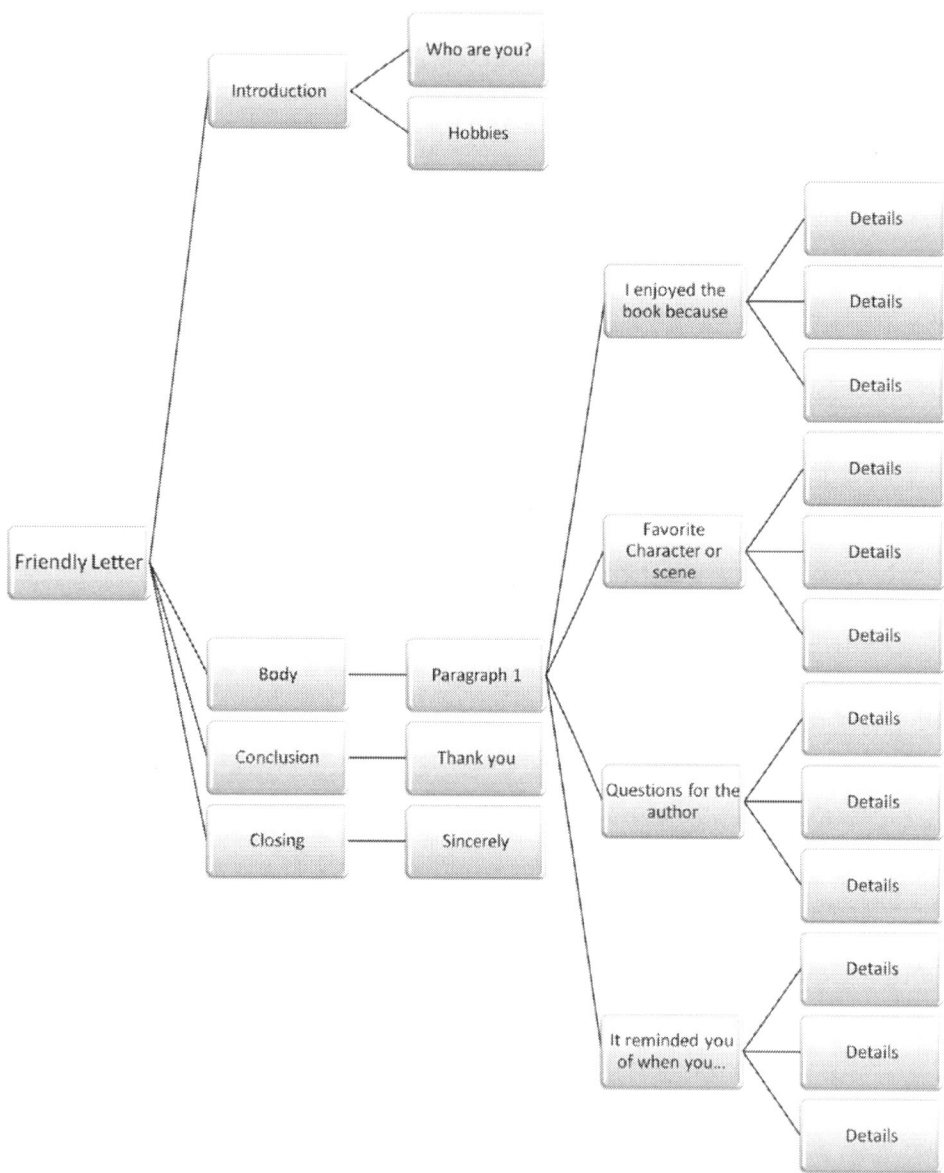

Figure 9 Friendly Letter Graphic Organizer

Use Clustering to Organize Writing

Writing an Effective Essay

Background:

Graphic organizers have been applied across a range of curriculum subject areas. Although reading is by far the most well studied application, science, social studies, language arts, and math are additional content areas that are represented in the research base on graphic organizers. In these subject areas, graphic organizers have been shown to have benefits that extend beyond their well-established effects on reading comprehension. Operations such as mapping cause and effect, note taking, comparing and contrasting concepts, organizing problems and solutions, and relating information to main ideas or themes can be broadly beneficial.(Ewy, 2003; Marzano, Pickering, Pollock, et al., 2001; Moore, 1984)

Learning Objectives:

- Organize an essay.
- Use specific topic sentences
- Use appropriate sentences to support the topic sentence in each paragraph

Application to Response to Intervention Tiers:

TIER ONE	TIER TWO	TIER THREE
Teacher uses strategy with entire class to differentiate instruction	Student(s) use a structured approach for writing a paragraph, essay or paper using the clustering structure. Student works with a peer tutor, specialist or in a coaching session with the classroom teacher at least twice per week until the study strategy is internalized.	Student works with a specialist one-to-one for an additional 60 to 90 minutes per week using this intervention as a strategy to facilitate increased skill in expressive writing.

Addresses the following non-responder indicators:

- Note taking deficiencies
- Attention Deficit Disorder
- Difficulty distinguishing the correct written word from the incorrect word
- Note taking deficiencies
- Difficulty organizing information

- Low clerical aptitude – difficulty completing written work
- Struggle to effectively use words to express organized and complete Thoughts in writing
- Word usage skills below standard
- Difficulty establishing writing goals – inattention and regulation problems when writing
- Gaps in instruction

Materials needed:
- Lined paper strips or lined sticky notes
- Scissors
- Scotch Tape

Approximate time frame for completion:
- Main lesson: two class periods
- Extension learning: Variable

Intervention Procedure & Scripts

Tier One/Whole Group (Introduction)

Clustering Activity Step One

a. Have your students draw a big circle on a piece of paper.

b. Put the topic of the paper in the center of the circle. Note: If there is more than one topic, you might have more than one circle. For example, writing about three wishes will require three circles: one for each wish.

c. Instruct your students to write any thoughts, ideas, or feelings about the topic in the circle. Students can also ask questions about the topic or draw pictures of ideas.

d. Do not worry about spelling, grammar, sentences, etc. at this point. The purpose is to get the ideas out. Worry about writing rules later.

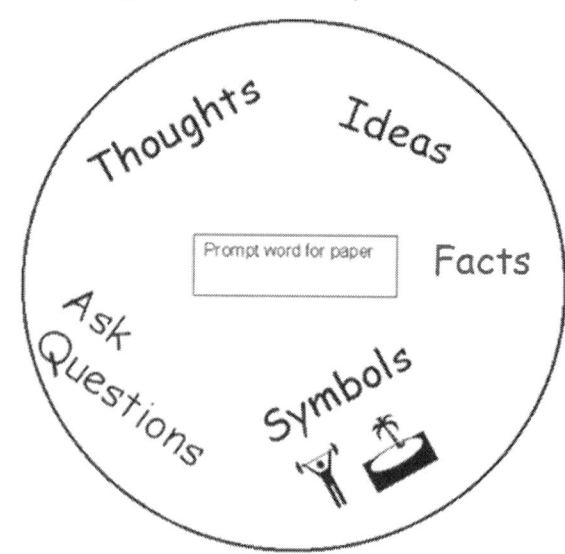

Make this circle BIG; at least the size of an 8" X 8" piece of paper.

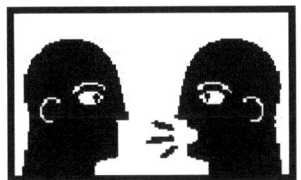

After students "create" in the circle, allow them to share what they have written with a partner.

Clustering Step Two

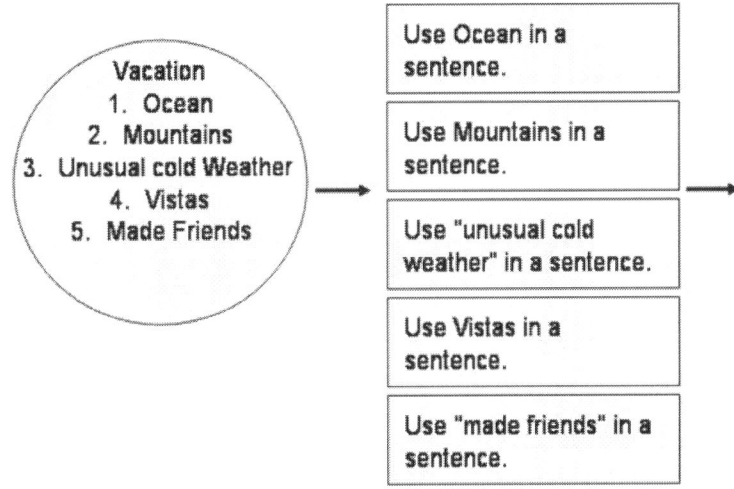

e. Instruct students to take the "best" words and ideas from inside their circle and use each word in a sentence.

f. These are the topic sentences for the paragraphs they will write.

g. Write the sentences on strips of lined notepaper or lined sticky notes.

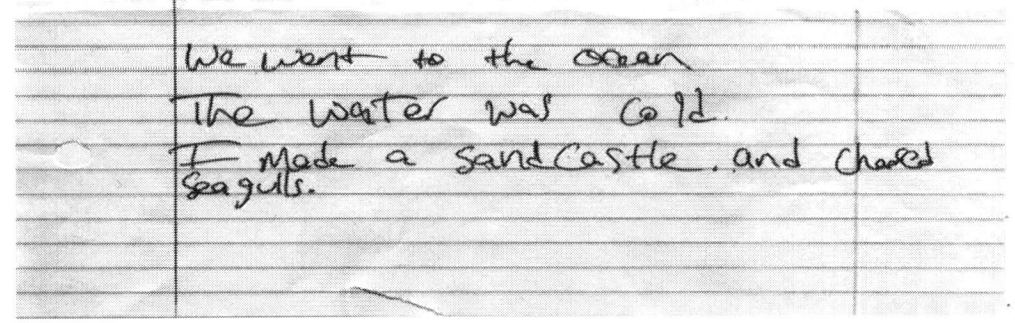

h. Now, take each sentence and add some more sentences about the topic sentence on that strip of paper.

i. Try to write two or three more sentences for each topic sentence.

*NOTE: Do not worry about spelling, grammar, or punctuation at this point in the exercise. Worrying about the rules makes it more difficult to be creative.

Clustering Step Three

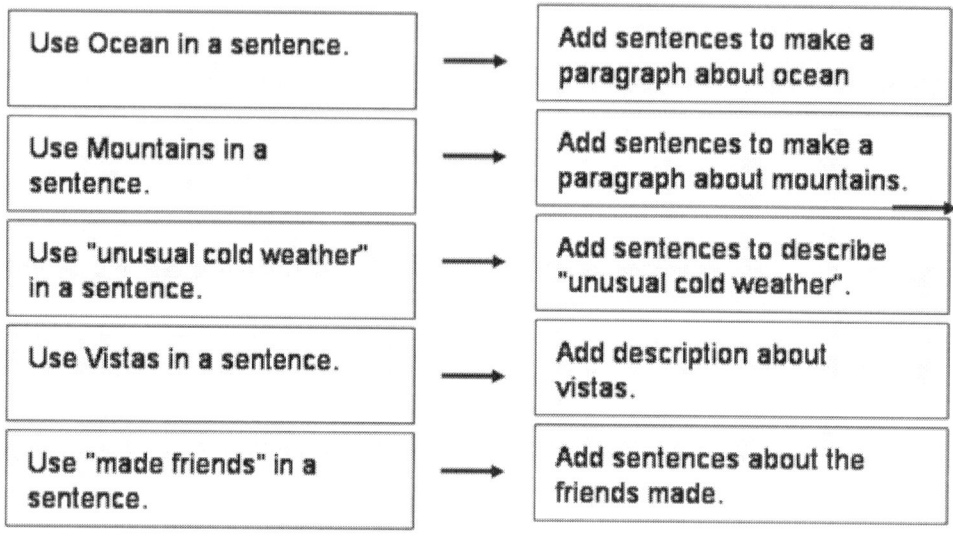

Clustering Step Four

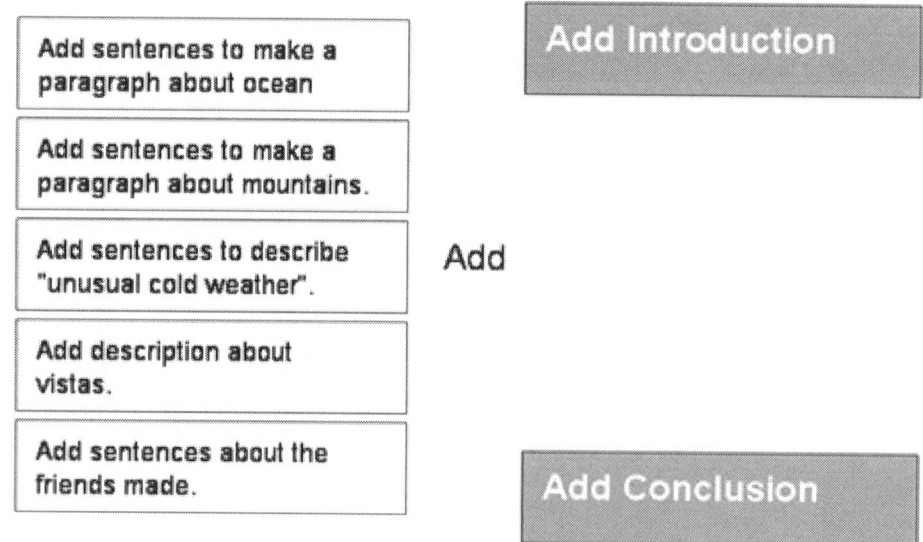

a. Next, add an introduction and conclusion on separate strips of lined paper.

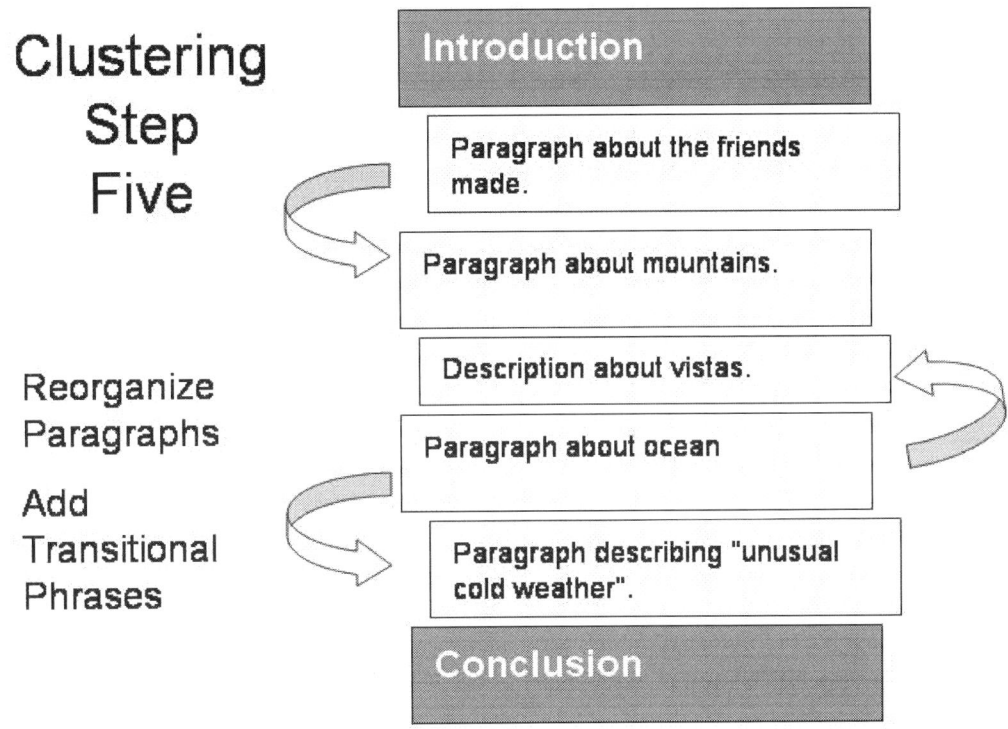

Clustering
Step
Five

Reorganize
Paragraphs

Add
Transitional
Phrases

Introduction

Paragraph about the friends made.

Paragraph about mountains.

Description about vistas.

Paragraph about ocean

Paragraph describing "unusual cold weather".

Conclusion

b. Next, move the strips of paper around so that they in the best order and make the most sense.

c. This process allows the writer to start anywhere in the paper. It frees up creative thought and encourages the process to start. Organizing the paper after paragraphs are written is easy.

d. Tape all the strips on one or two big pieces of paper.

e. Add transition words to make the paragraphs flow together.

Clustering Step Six

Rewrite or type into one continuous draft on full sheets of paper.

Hand in draft for teacher to correct.

Introduction
Paragraph about the friends made.
Paragraph about mountains.
Description about vistas.
Paragraph about ocean
Paragraph describing "unusual cold weather".
Conclusion

If the teacher is not correcting a draft, parents may be able to help with this step.

Clustering Step Seven

Student writes final draft incorporating teacher corrections, feedback and edits.

My Vacation   **By Successful Student**   **Interesting new friends became the focal point of ....**   **The mountains were...**   **The vistas were inspiring as mountains met the ocean in a clash of green and aquamarine...**   **Unfortunately there was an unusual cold weather front....**   **Overall, the vacation was...**

Across the Curriculum:

- Social Studies and Science teachers can use this strategy to help students write effective essays in their subject areas.
- Math teachers can use it to help students break down and explain multi-step problems.

Tier Two/Tier Three

*This is an excellent Tier Two & Tier Three practice activity.

1. Take all of the students' strips when they are complete.
2. Put each student's cluster strips in a separate baggie.
3. Put them into a center and have other students place them in order.
4. Have a copy of the finished essays so they can read them and see if they put them in the same order as the student that wrote the paper.

Assessment:

Clustering Rubric

CATEGORY	1	2	3	4
Neatness and Presentation	Illegible in many places, with many misspelled words, capitalization errors, and inappropriate spacing.	Messy in a few spots, with several words misspelled or not capitalized.	Neat and orderly in overall appearance, with few spelling and capitalization errors.	Exceptionally neat, orderly, and accurate.
Use of descriptive words	Lacks adjectives necessary for visualizing what is happening in the essay.	Good choice, but insufficient quantity of adjectives.	Descriptive adjectives help the reader to visualize what was happening in the essay.	Very descriptive adjectives help the reader to visualize what was happening in the essay.
Understanding	Unclear with lots of extraneous information.	Fairly clear, but supporting sentences do not support the topic sentence and disrupt the flow of the piece.	Clear, with most supporting sentences relevant to the topic sentence.	Clear with each paragraph containing a topic sentence supported by relevant sentences.

Transition Words

To Add:

And, again, and then, besides, equally important, finally, further, furthermore, nor, too, next, lastly, what's more, moreover, in addition, first (second, etc.)

To Compare:

Whereas, but, yet, on the other hand, however, nevertheless, on the other hand, on the contrary, by comparison, where, compared to, up against, balanced against, but, although, conversely, meanwhile, after all, in contrast, although this may be true

To Prove:

Because, for, since, for the same reason, obviously, evidently, furthermore, moreover, besides, indeed, in fact, in addition, in any case, that is

To Show Exception:

Yet, still, however, nevertheless, in spite of, despite, of course, once in a while, sometimes

To Show Time:

Immediately, thereafter, soon, after a few hours, finally, then, later, previously, formerly, first (second, etc.), next, and then

To Repeat:

In brief, as I have said, as I have noted, as has been noted

To Emphasize:

Definitely, extremely, obviously, in fact, indeed, in any case, absolutely, positively, naturally, surprisingly, always, forever, perennially, eternally, never, emphatically, unquestionably, without a doubt, certainly, undeniably, without reservation

To Show Sequence:

First, second, third, and so forth. A, B, C, and so forth. Next, then, following this, at this time, now, at this point, after, afterward, subsequently, finally, consequently, previously, before this, simultaneously, concurrently, thus, therefore, hence, next, and then, soon

To Give an Example:

For example, for instance, in this case, in another case, on this occasion, in this situation, take the case of, to demonstrate, to illustrate, as an illustration

To Summarize or Conclude:

In brief, on the whole, summing up, to conclude, in conclusion, as I have shown, as I have said, hence, therefore, accordingly, thus, as a result, consequently, on the whole

Part 2: Chapter 4:
Math Interventions

Bright Ideas

Model and Solve Equations Using Manipulatives

Background:

Using manipulatives provides students a meaningful context for mathematical knowledge and helps them understand fundamental relationships associated with the knowledge. Multiple embodiments – the use of many different models – allow students to focus on common characteristics and generalize to the abstract. ""Helping students make connections between the concrete (e.g., models and manipulatives) and the abstract (e.g. generalizations and symbolic representations) facilitates understanding, promotes success at learning, and helps relieve mathematics anxiety."(Reys, Lambdin, Lindquist, & Smith, 2009).

In regards to secondary math, such as Algebra, Henri Picciotti (Picciotto, 2010)writes:

> Even though they cannot make algebra easy, manipulatives can play an important role in the transition to a new algebra course:
> - They provide access to symbol manipulation for students who had previously been frozen out of the course because of their weak number sense.
> - They provide a geometric interpretation of symbol manipulation, thereby enriching all students' understanding, and making a powerful connection to another part of mathematics.
> - They support cooperative learning, and help improve discourse in the algebra class by giving students objects to think with and talk about. It is in the context of such reflection and conversation that learning happens.
>
> There are four main commercial versions of algebra manipulatives. In order of their appearance on the market, they are Algebra Tiles (Cuisenaire), the Lab Gear (Creative Publications), Algeblocks (Southwestern Publishing), and Algebra Models (Classroom Products). All four provide a worthwhile model of the distributive law. However, note that only the Lab Gear and Algeblocks allow work in three dimensions.

Learning Objectives:
- Use manipulatives and symbols to represent situations and solve problems
- Solve linear equations

Application to Response to Intervention Tiers:

TIER ONE	TIER TWO	TIER THREE
Teacher uses strategy with entire class to differentiate instruction	Pair students in same ability groups and provide ten minutes of intense coaching while other students are working on their own. See the following center application.	Same ability groups with direct, intense coaching by the teacher or math specialist. Student works with a specialist one-to-one for an additional 60 to 90 minutes per week using this intervention as a strategy to facilitate increased skill. See the following center application. Provide intense instruction one-on-one with a math intervention specialist using activities from the manipulative center.

Addresses the following non-responder indicators:
- Attention Deficit Disorder
- Difficulty with abstract concepts
- Inability to visualize math
- Difficulty following sequential procedures
- Limited strategic planning ability

Materials Needed:
- Balance scales
- Pennies or other tokens
- Rubber washers, toothpick rods, or small snack items.

Approximate time frame for completion:
Whole group instruction - 15 minutes
Centers and Small Groups – 10 to 12 minutes each

Intervention procedure & scripts:

Tier One/Whole group

Model on balance scale:
1. Put the same number of pennies or tokens on each side of the scale. Ask students what equation this represents ($n = n$).

2. Demonstrate that if you subtract the same amount from each side the scale remains balanced. For example, removing three pennies ($n - 3 = n - 3$) leaves the scale balanced

3. Place 10 pennies or tokens on each side of the scale. Demonstrate that removing a number of pennies from one side results in an imbalance on the scale. (Removing 5 from one side results in the equation $n - 5 < n$).

4. Remove 5 tokens from the other side of the scale to achieve a balance again. Then add 12 tokens to one side.

5. In order to make both sides balance again ($17 = x + ?$), add 1 penny at a time until the scale balances ($17 = x + 12$)..

6. Demonstrate how to prove x by subtracting 12 from both sides of the equation.

7. Model several problems like this. Illustrate the step-by-step solution on the board as you demonstrate the solution process using the scale as a visual example.

Tier One/Tier two: Partner Activity

1. After modeling to the whole group, assign students to a 'strategic partnership".
   - For <u>tier one</u>: Pair students in a mixed ability pair – high with middle, middle with low, etc.
   - For <u>tier two</u>: Pair students in same ability groups and provide ten minutes of intense coaching while other students are working on their own.

2. Use balance scales with pennies or tokens to practice solving simple linear equations ($x + 3 = 5$; $y + 7 = 9$; $n - 3 = 4$).

3. After students have had the opportunity to solve a selection of problems, bring them back together as a group and ask probing questions to ensure understanding and promote critical thinking
   - What did you have to do when you had a subtraction problem rather than an addition problem?

4. Discuss and reinforce the concept of adding or subtracting the same number from each side.

Centers Application for All Three Tiers

Tier One: Mixed ability groups

Tier Two: Same ability groups or Peer Tutoring

Tier Three: Same ability groups with direct, intense coaching by the teacher or math specialist.

Investigation Center
In this center, the students will begin to explore dividing both sides of an equation by the same number.

1. Give students a bag with a variety of different kinds of tokens. A sample bag would include: 5 of one item and 10 of another. (5 toothpicks and 10 rubber washers).

2. Tell students that the toothpicks and rubber washers are an equation and they need to find out how many rubber washers each toothpick is worth.
3. First, they are to write the equation ($5p = 10$), then solve it.
4. Have students model the solution of the equation by putting each toothpick on the table, then distributing the rubber washers. In this case, they would put out the 5 toothpicks. Then, after distributing the rubber washers, they would find that there are 2 rubber washers for each toothpick.
5. Model how to solve the equation by dividing both sides by 5.

Manipulative Center

1. Have students use a scale and tokens in the class to solve linear equations provided by the teacher

or

2. Use a virtual scale from a source like The National Library of Virtual Manipulatives (http://nlvm.usu.edu/en/nav/grade_g_4.html, scroll down to "Algebra Balance Scales") to model and solve linear equations.
3. Another great virtual manipulative website is GeoGebra.org.

<u>Tier Three:</u>

Provide intense instruction one-on-one with a math intervention specialist using activities from the manipulative center. Manipulatives, whether hands on or virtual, are critical to helping students who struggle with math concepts to gain an understanding. It is also important to allow adequate frequency and time for skill building. Some students simply need more processing time.

Assessment Center

Students show their understanding of linear equations by completing the attached problems. These problems are differentiated by complexity (one step problems, two-step problems, and challenge problems).

Application Examples:

One-Step Problems

$4 + x = 17$

$n - 9 = 13$

$3b = 21$

$12 + j = 19$

$7 - m = 2$

Two-Step Problems

$6n + 3 = 21$

$2p + 1 = -7$

$5m - 2 = 18$

$-4y + 3 = -13$

$-2z - 5 = -4$

Challenge Problems

$4x - 5 = 7x + 3$

$2(3n + 4) - (x - 3) = 36$

$3x - 1 = 2x + 7$

Rubric:

Connect Similarities and Differences between Literature and Student Lives

Category	1	2	3	4
Student uses manipulatives and symbols to represent situations and solve problems.	At the Teacher Center, student needs consistent support from teacher or peer to translate the items in the manipulative bags into linear equations, write the equations, and solve them.	At the Teacher Center, student can translate the items in the manipulative bags into linear equations, write the equations, and solve them, with teacher support.	At the Teacher Center, student can translate the items in the manipulative bags into linear equations and write the equations with minimal teacher direction. Student can solve the equations independently and accurately.	At the Teacher Center, student can independently translate the items in the manipulative bags into linear equations, write the equations, and solve them accurately.
Student solves linear equations.	Student needs support to solve the 1-step problems on the practice sheet accurately.	Student can solve through the 1-step problems on the practice sheet independently and accurately; needs support for 2-step problems and above.	Student can solve through the 2-step problems on the practice sheet independently and accurately.	Student can solve through the "challenge" level problems on the practice sheet independently and accurately.

Math Vocabulary

The lesson plan samples and strategy examples in the chapter focused on vocabulary provide excellent examples for how to reinforce math vocabulary. Rather than create a separate lesson plan for math vocabulary, I'd like to share an example I saw effectively demonstrated at Permian High School in Odessa, Texas.

Ms. McAnnelly and Ms. Pettus, co-teachers at the tenth grade level, made vocabulary review part of their teaching practice. One of the techniques they used was to choose a state test question and spend five minutes a class period, usually at the end of class, reviewing the vocabulary in that item. They did not spend any time working out the math. They only focused on the vocabulary.

They presented a test question via laptop and projector on a screen. Each student had an index card. They were to review the question presented and list any words that they did not understand on that index card. Given that the class had a large bilingual population, this was an especially important exercise. The teachers collected the index cards as the students finished. They then used the information on the cards to drive vocabulary instruction throughout the semester.

In addition to having students list the words on an index card, they discussed the question with the class as a whole. I was fascinated to learn that the students found the question phrase, "Which of the following best represents . . ." the most challenging part of the test item. We tend to focus on math skills in preparation for state tests in math, however, we also need to concentrate on vocabulary. Many students may do poorly on the test because of a lack of vocabulary understanding rather than a lack of math skill.

It's important to teach math vocabulary to all students. It's critical for non-responders.

Also, teach students to look for clue words in math word problems.

- Clue words for addition: *sum, total, in all, perimeter*

- Clue words for subtraction: *difference, how much more, exceed*

- Clue words for multiplication: *product, total, area, times*

- Clue words for division: *share, distribute, quotient, average*

De-Clutter the Math[5]

One thing we must address when discussing math is that disorganized workspaces clutter up working memory. (Levine, 2003)This is because students are too busy trying to make order out of chaos to focus on the actual math problem. One of the best ways we can help students with math is to help them organize their workspace.(Levine, 2003)

- Write down the steps to the problem before solving it.
- Avoid mental arithmetic: Use a scratch pad or scrap paper.
- Use graph or lined paper to complete math problems
     a. Give your students grid paper or have them turn their **lined paper sideways**.
     b. Fold their lined paper into squares and do one problem in each square.
     c. Have students work their problems by lining the numbers up in the columns.
     d. When testing or doing math worksheets on plain paper, put a piece of dark lined paper or grid paper under the math page. Students will be able to see the lines through the page and will keep their math organized.
     e. If they become overwhelmed by looking at the entire test page, have students use blank paper to cover up everything but the problem they are working on so they don't become stressed. When they don't have to look at everything at once, they can focus more productively.

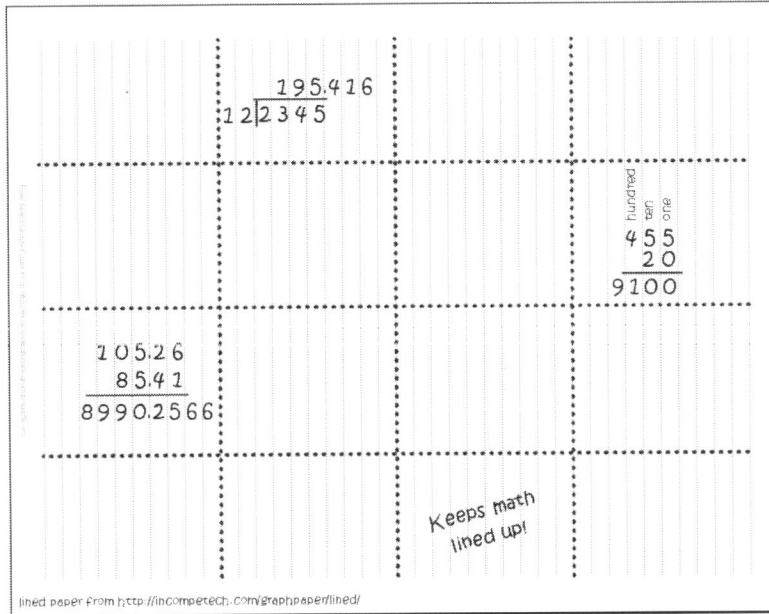

lined paper from http://incompetech.com/graphpaper/lined/

When students are working to organize their workspace or trying to decipher their work, they are using up working memory on organization rather than the math process. These strategies allow them to focus on the math.

---

[5] Memorization and Test Taking Strategies for the Differentiated, Inclusive and RTI Classroom by Susan Gingras Fitzell, Cogent Catalyst Publications, 2010

Part 2: Chapter 5:
Interventions for Recall & Recognition

Bright Ideas

Intervention Strategies for Increasing Recall & Recognition[6]

Many students with learning disabilities struggle with memory deficits. Primarily, they forget information they need to do well on tests or to do the higher-level thinking required for problem solving, analysis, and synthesis. For example, if students can't remember basic math facts, even if they have a calculator at their disposal, they will take longer to complete a test, thereby impacting their test scores.(Levine, 2003)

Working memory space for these students is being used up with basic calculations rather than higher-level thinking skills. Students who struggle to remember the details of a story can't draw inferences from those details because they can't remember the sequence of events or what happened at various parts of the story.

Remembering the details and foundation of what is being taught is critical to comprehending, applying, and analyzing what is being taught. A **Tier-Two intervention strategy** to differentiate instruction for students struggling to remember information in the classroom is to teach short-term memory strategies.

Teach Students to **Chunk Information**: (Miller)

The brain can only hold seven pieces of information at a time in short-term memory. The only way we can sometimes get away with more than seven facts is if we 'chunk' related information by color. So, if we have eight or nine things, we might be able to use color to make it more like seven if some of those things go together.

For example, five facts about short-term memory might be green, five facts about working memory could be brown, and five facts about long-term memory could be black. We chunk related information by color.

Paraphrase Immediately(Shugarman, 1986)
Another strategy to enhance short-term memory so information isn't "gone" in two seconds is to have a student paraphrase what we just taught. (Shugarman, 1986)For example, after you've taught something important, ask a volunteer to paraphrase that information for the class. Most likely, your students will not relate the information in the same words you used, which will be novel to the brain. This strategy only takes seconds to do, yet it lets your students hear the information again, in a different way, with a different voice. The brain likes novelty and will remember the information better.

Paraphrase One Hour Later

---

[6] Memorization and Test Taking Strategies for the Differentiated, Inclusive and RTI Classroom by Susan Gingras Fitzell, Cogent Catalyst Publications, 2010

Ask your students to paraphrase information that was shared earlier in the day. When they take something you taught an hour ago and bring it back into play, it returns to short-term memory and is then pushed into working memory. Using this paraphrasing strategy in your classrooms will help students to remember what you are teaching.

Whisper It

Rehearsal is a strategy(Levine, 2003) that we've been using in education for years. One rehearsal strategy is to have students stop after you've shared an important fact and whisper the important information three times. The repetition and the whispering help them to remember the fact. Whispering under one's breath is a powerful tool.

Make a Rulebook

One of the best ways to help kids remember rules is to make a 'rulebook'(Levine, 2003)for your subject.

1. Use two-column pages and split the rules for clarity.
2. Label one column "If" and the other column "Then."
    a. For example, in the If column, we might say, "I before E", while the Then column would say, "Except after C".
    b. You can do this for most subject areas.

Applying rules is a fairly simple strategy, as long as the rule is clear. For example, some of us learned the months of the year with a rhyme and some of us learned a physical rule using our knuckles. These are memory strategies focused on rules that we have used all our lives, and still use.

Reflection Notes

Part 2 Chapter 6:
Intervention Strategies that Work Across the Curriculum

Bright Ideas

Intervention Strategies that Work Across the Curriculum

There are several challenges to writing a text that is both research-based and uses language that fosters the credibility of the author, yet does not get jargon-based and so academic that we lose the reader. For example, I just read this phrase in some research, "...students will have the metacognitive foundation for extracting and constructing meaning from [fill in your source of choice] with automaticity." What does that really mean? Well, if I research the definition of metacognition, I quickly determine that the research is not definitive and the descriptions vary. Several sources state that it is very difficult to define metacognition. Rather, it is easier to give examples of it. I'm of that same mindset. I'd prefer to avoid educational jargon and speak a common language that we might speak in the classroom when working with our students. I consider myself a teacher's teacher and consequently, feel passionate about providing information to teachers that is easily implemented, grounded common sense and do-able.

For every strategy presented in this book, I will present the strategy as it would be used in Tier One as a Differentiated Instruction strategy. Then I will share how it might be used at Tier Two and Three. At the secondary level, it's important for students to make these strategies their own. Consequently, we will address these strategies not only as they might be used by the teacher, but also by the student.

Identify Similarities & Differences

Background:
When teachers use activities that engage students in identifying similarities and differences, students achieve percentile gains of up to 46 percent as a result of resulting proficiency. (Marzano, Pickering, & Pollock, 2001)

Learning objectives:
- To distinguish the characteristics of printed materials based on comparative observation.
- To create analogies between characters in a piece of literature and characters in students' everyday lives, thus incorporating more than one layer of connection to enhance long-term memory and critical thinking skills.
- To engage the student in higher-ordered learning processes involving differentiation and analysis.

Application to Response to Intervention Tiers:

TIER ONE	TIER TWO	TIER THREE
Teacher uses strategy with entire class to differentiate instruction	Student(s) use a structured form to identify similarities as they read assigned novels. Student works with a peer tutor, specialist or in a coaching session with the classroom teacher at least twice per week until the study strategy is internalized.	Student works with a specialist one-to-one for an additional 60 to 90 minutes per week using this intervention as a strategy to facilitate reading recall, comprehension and analysis.

Addresses the following non-responder indicators:

- Attention deficit disorder
- Inability to connect new information with previously learned knowledge
- Inability to activate prior knowledge; difficulty retrieving information learned
- Trouble remembering what the teacher says in class
- Poor auditory short-term memory
- Inability to recode incoming information into meaningful information
- Difficulty with higher order thinking such as problem solving and comparing and contrasting
- Difficulty processing information in a way that is meaningful to them.

Materials needed:

Literature, a short story, etc.

- Social Studies teachers might consider using key characters in a historical story.
- Science teachers might use this approach when studying concepts that have a human element. For example, the activists on both sides of a land use issue, stem cell research, or green energy vs. fossil fuels.

Randy Anderson

Johnny Cade

Darrel (Darry) Curtis

Ponyboy Curtis

Sodapop Curtis

Paul Holden

Johnnycakes

Marcia

Two-bit Matthews

Keith Matthews

Buck Merrill

Steve Randle

Sandy

Bob Sheldon

Curley Shepard

Tim Shepard

Mr. Syme

Cherry Valance

Sherri valance

Dally Winston

Jerry Wood

The Outsiders: What peer group would they be hanging with at our school?

Approximate time frame for completion:

- Creating the analogy – 10 minutes
- Resulting discussion or extension learning – variable

Intervention Procedure & Scripts

1. Give students any of the following:
   a. Characters from a short story
   b. Characters from a novel (e.g.: The Outsiders)
   c. Key people discussed in a textbook that represent a period of time.
2. List the characters on the board[7] or have students list the characters through a small group brainstorm.
3. Tell students to draw correlations between the characters on the list and people in their life.
4. Once students have determined parallels between characters on the list and people in their own life, have them GROUP the characters based on common features, personalities, politics, ideology, etc.
5. Using Venn diagrams, or graphic organizers (see Figure 10 Similarities **& Differences**) list similarities and differences between the groups in the story/text/historical period and groups they have personal experience with today.
6. Have students create stick figure/line drawing representations of the differences between the groups.

---

[7] The "board" is an all-encompassing term for Overhead Projector, SmartBoard, StarBoard, White Board, Chalk Board, LCD, etc.

Application Example:

Across the United States, seventh and eighth graders read S.E. Hinton's *The Outsiders*. The book, set in the 1950's, has relevance for today's youth, however, to youth of the millennium, the 1950's may seem to be ancient history.

Here's an example of how we might differentiate instruction at Tier One, as well as use best practice researched based strategies as an intervention for students who have difficulty with reading comprehension, reading recall and analytical thinking.

1. List the characters from *The Outsiders* on the board.
2. Ask students to imagine that the characters from the book are their age and in their grade.
3. Ask students to identify where they might be hanging out at school and who might they be hanging with if they were the 'Greasers' or the 'Socks.' Where might a 13-year-old Mr. Syme hang out?
4. List their 'pairs' on the board.
5. Now that students have categorized and paired the book character with someone from their peer group and social world, ask students to compare and contrast the characters and their peer groups. "How are the greasers the same as _____ from our school? How are they different from students here?"

To differentiate:

1. Group students in mixed ability triads to list similarities and differences.
2. Allow students choices:
   a. Illustrate the differences between characters then and now by creating meaningful symbols to represent the differences.
   b. Create analogies using the characters:
   c. Pony boy is to _____ as _____ is to _____.
   d. Greasers is to Socks as _____ is to _____

Across the curriculum:

For Social Studies instruction, take the topic of immigration. In *U. S. History and History Standards for Grades 5-12* Standard two is, "Massive immigration after 1870 and how new social patterns, conflicts, and ideas of national unity developed amid growing cultural diversity." One of the strands in this standard is to assess the challenges, opportunities, and contributions of different immigrant groups.

Have students identify:
- The new students in their school.
- New communities in their city, region or state.
- Any relatives or friends who immigrated to the United States

How are today's "new kids in town" the same as immigrants from the late 1800's? How might they be different? Were opportunities the same or different? (See **Figure 11 Similarities & Differences Study Form)**

Assessment:

Rubric: Connect Similarities and Differences between Literature and Student Lives

Category	1	2	3	4
Similarities and Differences s	Misses similarities or differences between characters in the text and individuals or groups in his/her personal world.	Broadly notes, but does not elaborate on similarities or differences between characters in the text to individuals or groups in his/her personal world.	Elaborates on similarities or differences between characters in the text to individuals or groups in his/her personal world.	Expands upon the analogies to draw parallels between the two worlds and deepen understanding of the characters in the literature piece.
Likenesses and Differences From Specific People or Groups in Students' Lives.	Does not specify or detail clear similarities and differences between characters in the text to people in his/her personal world.	Specifies and details clear similarities and differences between characters in the text to people in his/her personal world but does not elaborate on those differences.	Elaborates on similarities and differences between characters in the text to people in his/her personal world.	Expands upon the analogies to explain how the details in the literature piece are similar to the details of the lives of people in the student's personal world and why that correlation is significant to understanding the literature, history, etc.

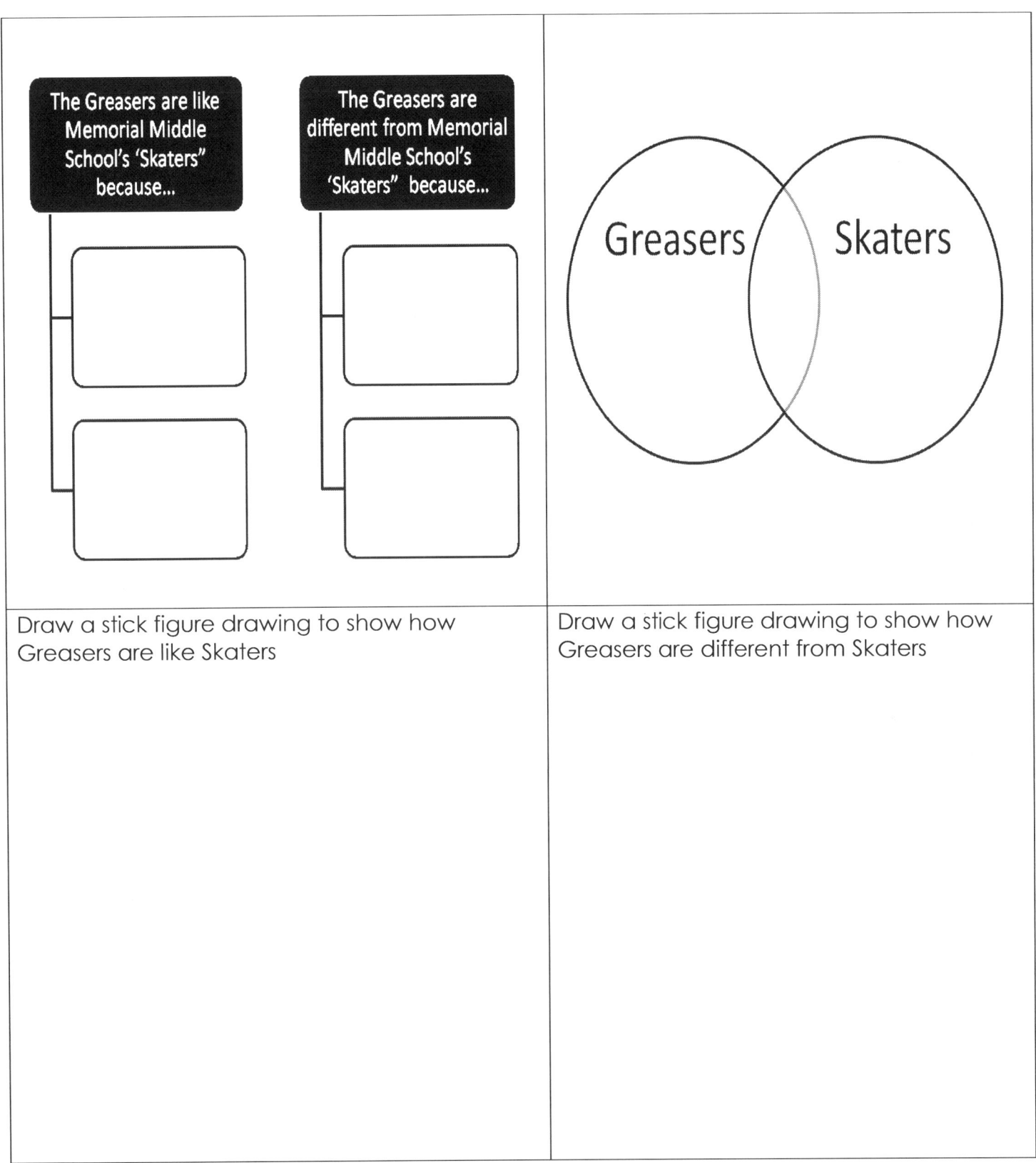

Figure 10 Similarities & Differences

Student/Team Name:_____

Similarities & Differences Study Form

The two topics being compared are:
_____ and _____

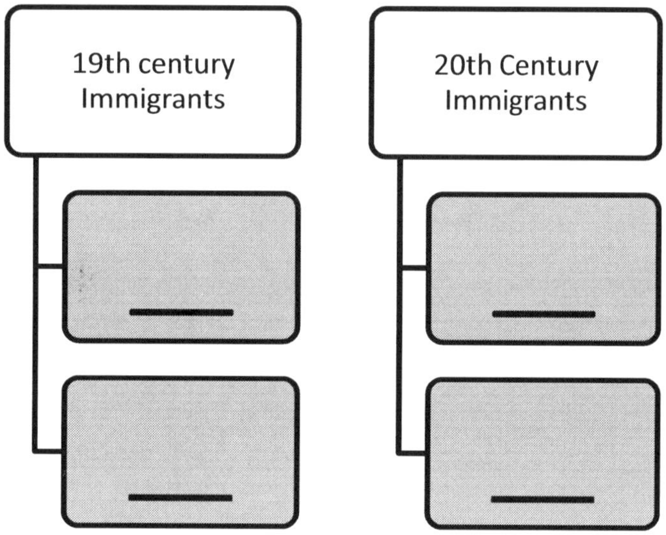

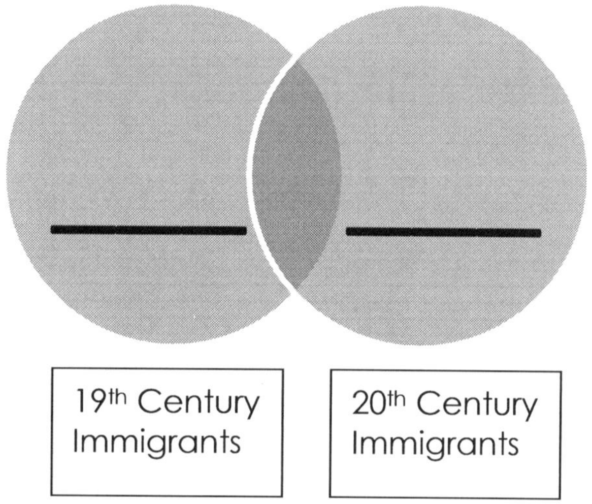

19th century
Immigrants

20th Century
Immigrants

_____

_____

_____

_____

19th Century
Immigrants

20th Century
Immigrants

Draw a stick figure drawing to help you remember how _____ are alike.

Draw a stick figure drawing to help you remember how _____ are different.

Optional for Bonus points: Create a song, rhyme or rap that sings about the similarities and differences

Figure 11 Similarities & Differences Study Form

Mind Mapping / Graphic Roadmaps / Visual Organizers

Background:

Developing cognitive maps and using advance organizers increases critical thinking skills. (Barba and Merchant 1990; Snapp and Glover 1990; Tierney, et al. 1989).

Long-term memory files information in the brain through patterns, procedures, categories, pairs, and rules. A mind map uses at least three of these five ways to store information. A classic mind map begins with a word, phrase, or idea typically placed in the center of a piece of paper. Then, as the author of the mind map expands upon the word or phrase in the middle, the mind map expands to include various ideas that come to mind when considering that center prompt.

Mind maps enable the brain to categorize information. A mind map is a non-linguistic representation method of organizing information that enables students to file information away in long-term memory in multiple modes or memory packets.

Figure 12 Visual Organizers

Students learn and remember mind maps better if they create them out of their own mental images and patterns. As a parent who has spent my children's lifetimes trying to teach them how to learn, I was very excited when I walked into my daughter's college apartment and found mind-maps, mnemonics, color, etc. all over one of her walls. Now, it's not unusual to find mandalas on her door or on her walls, or flash cards scattered about, but this was a huge mind-map made from recycled 8.5 X 11 inch pieces of paper. (**See Figure 12 Visual Organizers**) I had to take a picture. I had no idea what it all meant, but I do know it helped her to get an A in the course. My daughter, Shivahn, co-wrote a book with me, *Umm...Studying? What's That?* So it's reassuring to know that she didn't 'just' write the book, she also uses the strategies and shares them with other teens.

Learning objectives:

- To improve recall of data
- To incorporate multiple modes of storing information in long-term memory so that all types of learners can be successful.
- To create meaningful connections between previously learned information, new information, and connected information.
- To categorize, create paired associations, incorporate non-linguistic representation and critical thinking skills into the learning process.

Application to Response to Intervention Tiers:

TIER ONE	TIER TWO	TIER THREE
Teacher uses strategy with entire class to differentiate instruction	Student(s) use mind mapping (with or without mind mapping software, or mapping handout) as they read assigned novels. Student works with a peer tutor, specialist or in a coaching session with the classroom teacher at least twice per week until the study strategy is internalized.	Student works with a specialist one-to-one for an additional 60-90 minutes per week using this intervention as a strategy to facilitate reading comprehension, critical thinking and recall.

Addresses the following non-responder indicators:

- Difficulty focusing, planning, and organization.
- Difficulty connecting new information with previously learned knowledge
- Difficulty activating prior knowledge; difficulty retrieving information learned
- Difficulty remembering what the teacher says in class
- Poor auditory short-term memory
- Difficulty recoding incoming information into meaningful connections
- Difficulty with higher order thinking such as problem solving, sequencing, organizing thoughts into a meaningful pattern
- Difficulty categorizing information, pairing information, formulating associations when reading or writing.
- Difficulty writing a paragraph, or essay.
- Difficulty seeing patterns in math problems

Materials needed:

- Chart paper and crayons/markers OR Copy paper and color pencils/markers/gel pens
- Sample mind maps on another topic to provide a model / example

- Text book, literature, class notes, or other source of content to be mind mapped

Approximate time frame for completion:
- Creating the mind map – 10 minutes or longer
- Resulting discussion or extension learning –variable

Intervention procedure & scripts
First, explain what a mind map is. (See **Figure 13 Social Studies Mind Map & Figure 14 Science Mind Map**)

For independent writing assignments:
1. Ask students:
   - to contribute words that come to mind when they think of __(the topic)__ to be written about;
   - what images come to mind when they think about ___(the topic)___.
2. Tell students to list their ideas around the topic using the mind map format to create logical connections.
3. Enhance the mind map with stick figure images, color, and meaningful symbols.

For independent reading assignments (literature or content area):
1. Ask students:
   - to pull key words from their reading: events, characters, dates tied to something meaningful (list both together), places, cause & effect, etc.;
   - what images come to mind when they think about these key words.
2. Tell students to list their ideas around the topic using the mind map format to create logical connections.
3. Enhance the mind map with stick figure images, color, and meaningful symbols.

For group brainstorming and mind map creation:
Break into groups of three and continue with steps 2-4 above. Avoid groups of more than four.

Extension - making more of the mind map
Students may illustrate the ideas on their mind map by placing photographs, illustrations, and links to relevant websites.

For example, they can:

- Take photographs to illustrate their ideas using the digital camera and upload them.
- Scan photographs and pictures out of books and magazines.
- Copy quotes from literature, magazines or newspapers, which are relevant to the topic.
- Write up quotes from the class discussion.

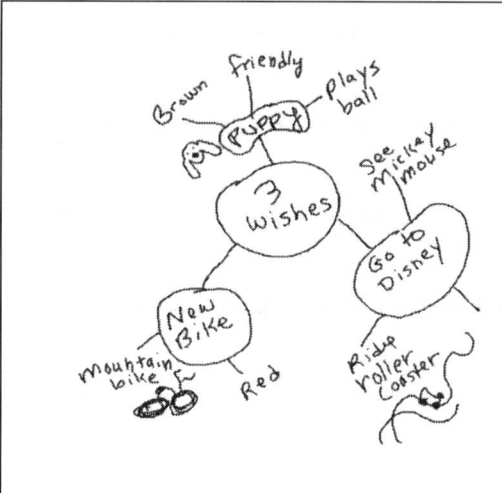

Note:
When students make spelling errors at this phase of the creative process, note them, but let them go. Correcting students' spelling while they are creating will cause them to clutter their working memory with rules and not allow enough "space" for coming up with ideas. So, correct the difference between 'add' and 'ad' later.

Application Example:

Writing in the content area: Social Studies

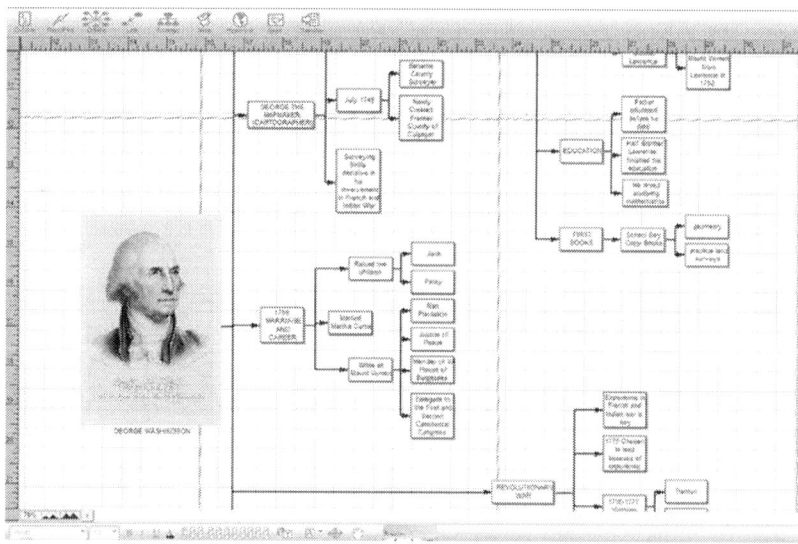

Figure 13 Social Studies Mind Map

A student created the above mind map as the 'outline' of his paper and presentation on George Washington's life and accomplishments.

Application example:

Independent reading in the content area: Science

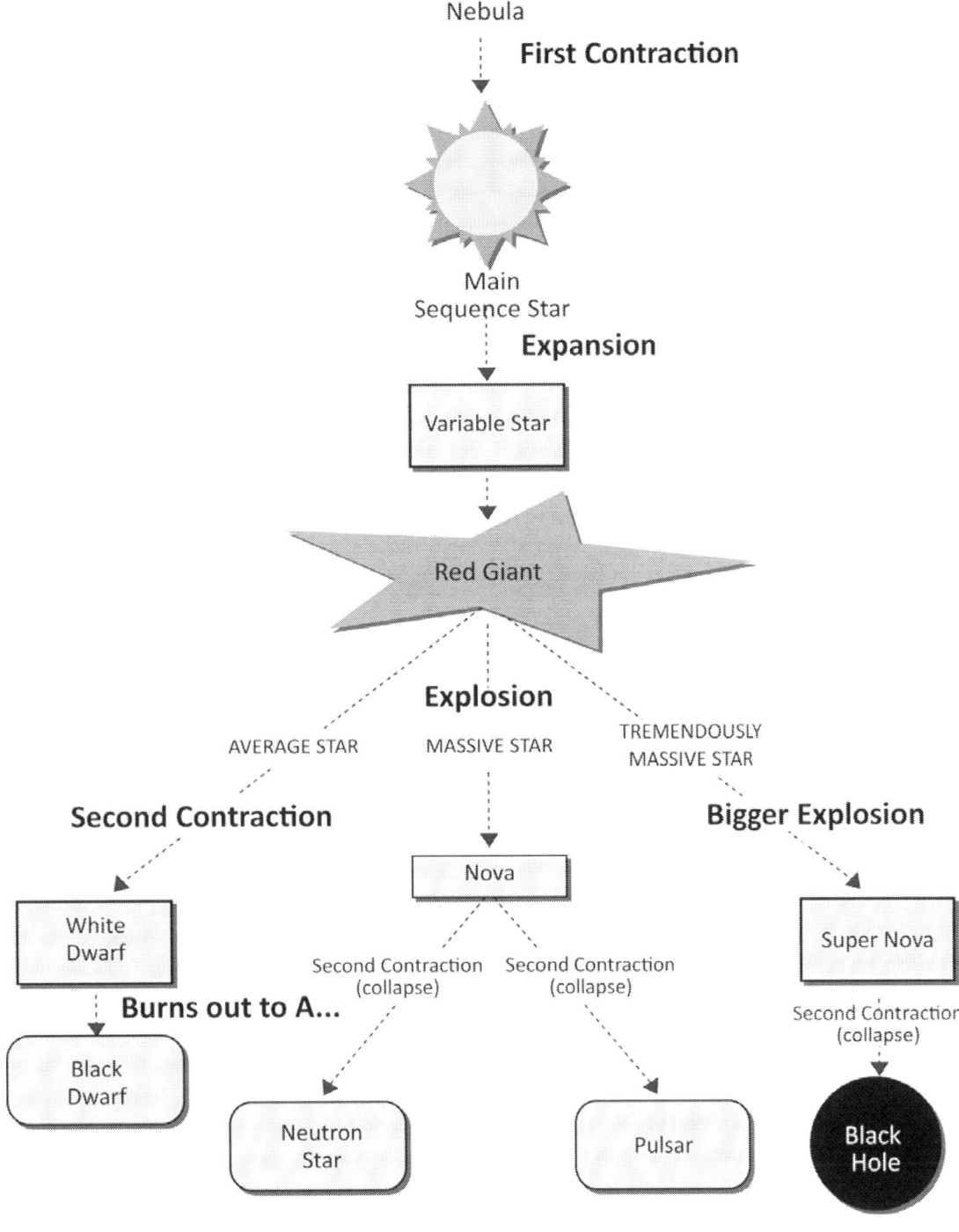

Figure 14 Science Mind Map

Assessment:

Mind Map Rubric

Category	1	2	3	4
Neatness and Presentation	The mind map is not neat enough to understand.	The mind map is not neat enough to understand most concepts	The mind map is well presented and most of the information is easy to understand	The mind map is well presented and all the information is easy to understand
Use of Images and Symbols	The mind map includes few images	The mind map includes some images	Some categories are enhanced with simple symbols or diagrams.	Most categories are enhanced with simple symbols or diagrams.
Use of color	The mind map lacks color.	Uses color, but not to categorize throughout the mind map.	Color demonstrates some connections and or topics throughout the mind map.	Uses color to show all connections and/or to categorize topics throughout the mind map.
Understanding	The mind map includes 2 or fewer elements for each category.	The mind map includes at least 2 elements demonstrating comprehension for some categories,	The mind map contains 3 elements for some categories	The mind map contains at least 3 elements for each category.

Strategy to Remember Sequences

Some students struggle to remember sequences. They cannot remember a time line in history, the storyline in a short story, the steps to solve a geometric proof, or the sequence of a cycle in science. (Levine, 2003)How might we support students in recalling sequences? One approach is to make the sequence visually concrete.

Learning Objectives:

- To provide a recall strategy incorporating graphics created by the student in a specific, sequential fashion.
- To improve recall of data, for which proper sequencing is required.
- To incorporate multiple modes of storing information in long-term memory so that all types of learners can be successful.

- To create meaningful connections between new information and visual cues (non-linguistic representation) to enable students to remember sequential information in the correct order.
- To categorize, create paired associations, incorporate non-linguistic representation and critical thinking skills into the learning process.

Application to Response to Intervention Tiers:

TIER ONE	TIER TWO	TIER THREE
Teacher uses strategy with entire class to differentiate instruction	Student(s) use sequencing strategy as they read assigned text. Student works with a peer tutor, specialist or in a coaching session with the classroom teacher at least twice per week until the study strategy is internalized.	Student works with a specialist one-to-one for an additional 60-90 minutes per week using this intervention as a strategy to facilitate reading comprehension, sequencing and recall.

Addresses the following non-responder indicators:
- Inability to arrange information to use it effectively.
- Difficulty focusing, planning, and organizing.
- Difficulty retrieving information learned in correct sequence.
- Difficulty remembering what the teacher says in class.
- Poor auditory short-term memory
- Inability re-code incoming information into meaningful connections
- Difficulty with higher order thinking such as problem solving, sequencing, and organizing thoughts into a meaningful pattern.
- Difficulty remembering the steps to solving a math problem, researching a hypothesis, timelines, cycles in science, or remembering the steps to any given task.

Materials needed:
- Adding machine or cash register tape
- Color pencils / markers / gel pens
- Sample sequence strips on another topic to provide model/example
- Textbook, literature, class notes, or other source of content to be sequenced.

Approximate time frame for completion:
- Creating the sequence strip – at least 10 minutes
- Resulting discussion or extension learning - variable

Intervention procedure & scripts

Explain what a sequence strip is. See Figure 15 Example of a Sequence Strip

Phase One:

1. Give students adding machine or cash register tape.
2. Choose text, note, timeline, or process that students will be sequencing.
3. Provide instruction (read aloud, review notes, present new information, etc.) to students and when a key fact, event, cause and effect, vocabulary word, date, etc. is presented:
   a. Stop
   b. Tell students to take their writing utensil and paper tape in hand
   c. Ask them what was important in what you just presented or read
   d. Verify the correct information, and then summarize it into a KEY WORD which will become the label for that information on the paper tape
   e. Draw a stick figure representation of that information on the board
   f. Students should copy the teacher's drawing on their paper strip, or they may create their own image (what is critical is that the image is meaningful to the student)
   g. Students should have a picture with a label. (See Figure 15 Example of a Sequence Strip
   h. Continue this process until students have a completed sequence strip highlighting the most important concepts, connections, cause and effect situations, etc. outlined on their paper tape

Phase two:

After students become familiar with the technique and competent in using the strategy independently, advance to the following options:

Option 1:

a) While providing instruction in class, repeat steps a-d above, however, ONLY write down the KEY WORD or phrase (label).
b) Have students draw a picture for each label for homework or independent practice. This ensures that they will have to revisit the information again. Do not allow too much time between the verbal component and the drawing component. Ideally, students will draw pictures approximately 3-6 hours later. This gap in time is the first step to moving the information from short-term memory to working memory.

Option 2:

a) Students work independently, in pairs, or in triads.
b) As students are reading a textbook or story, instruct them to draw pictures of the important information (characters, historical figures, places, events, etc.) in the order that they appear in the information source (text, sequence, instructions, timeline, process, etc.) on adding machine tape starting at the beginning of the tape and working left to right.
c) Have models available as visual reminders for students.

Application example:

Social Studies:

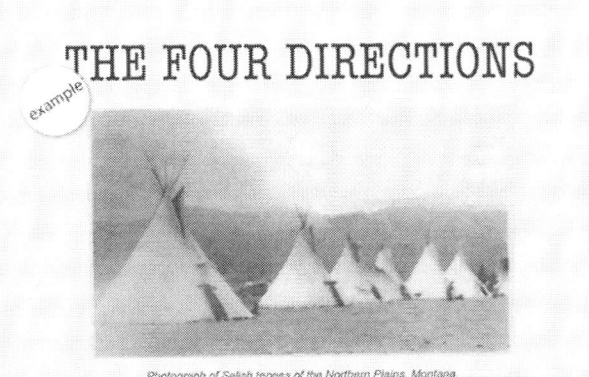

THE FOUR DIRECTIONS

Photograph of Salish tepees of the Northern Plains, Montana.

In the past, directions were part of the native way of life. the lakota (luh-KO-tuh), a tribe from the plains, faced their teppes to the east. Some tribes in Montana were taught to sleep by laying their heads to the north. These tribes were known as the Salish (SAY-lish). To get from one place to the next has been part of native living for a long time.

MEDICINE WHEELS

The circle has great part of the culture in the Northwest. Tribes of the plains had a type of circle called a **medicine wheel**. This wheel is a spiritual symbol to the tribes of the plains. It was used to teach the four cardinal direction.

The Lakota tribe used another kind of medicine wheel, too. Rocks were placed in a huge circle to form an outer rim. Stones were then lined up from the center to the circle's edge in many directions.

While your students read about how the Lakota Indians used directions for navigation, they draw a picture of the key points on the tape.

The chapter continues to describe what types of information was recorded by Native Americans such as the position of the sun and the moon, neighboring sites, etc.

Students draw and label that information in the same sequence/order that it is listed or described in the textbook. See the following example Figure 15 Example of a Sequence Strip

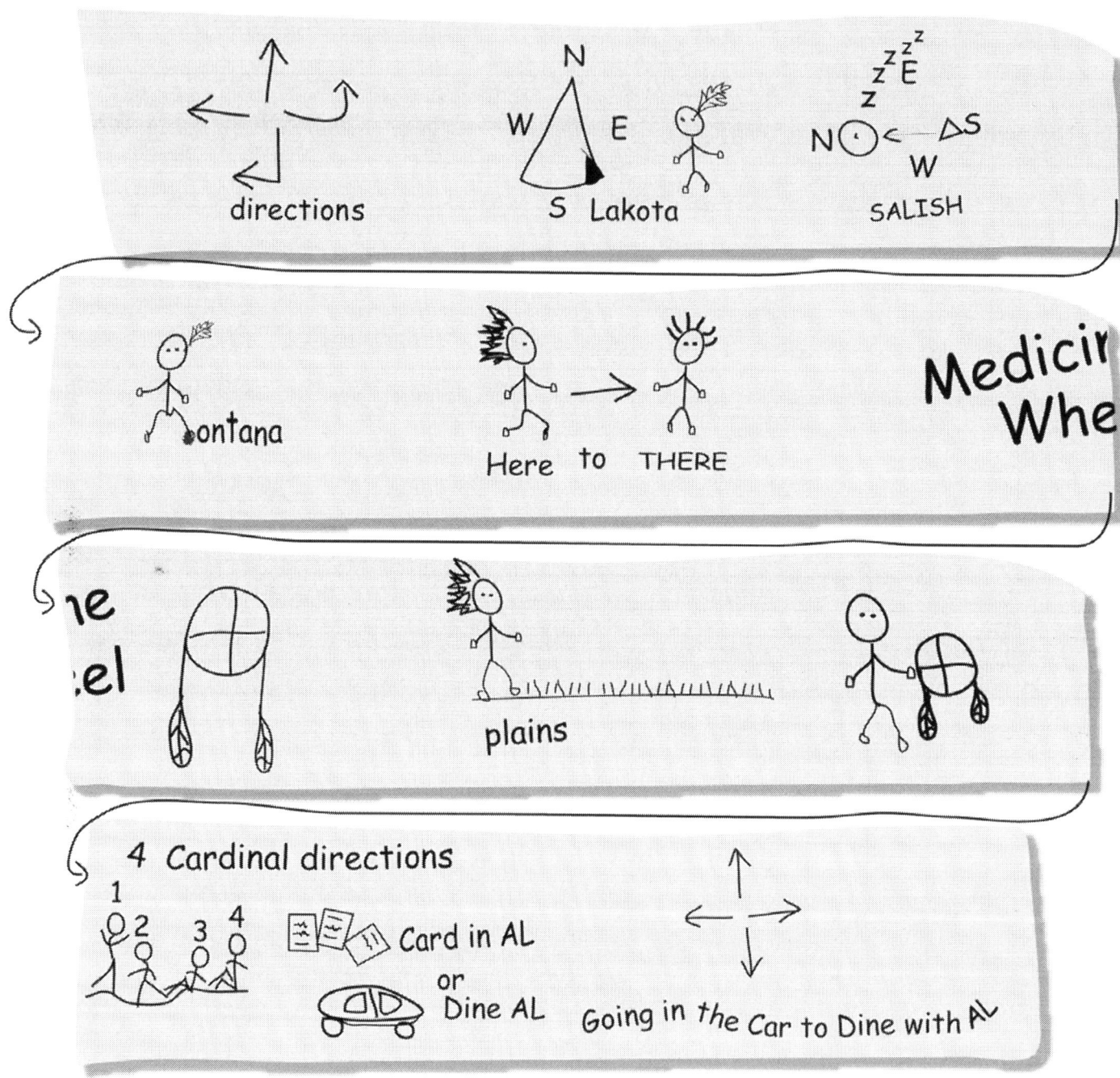

Figure 15 Example of a Sequence Strip

When complete, the student has a "time line" or "story line," in sequential order, of the events in the textbook or story. This visual memory tool will help them to remember the information in the order that it "happened".

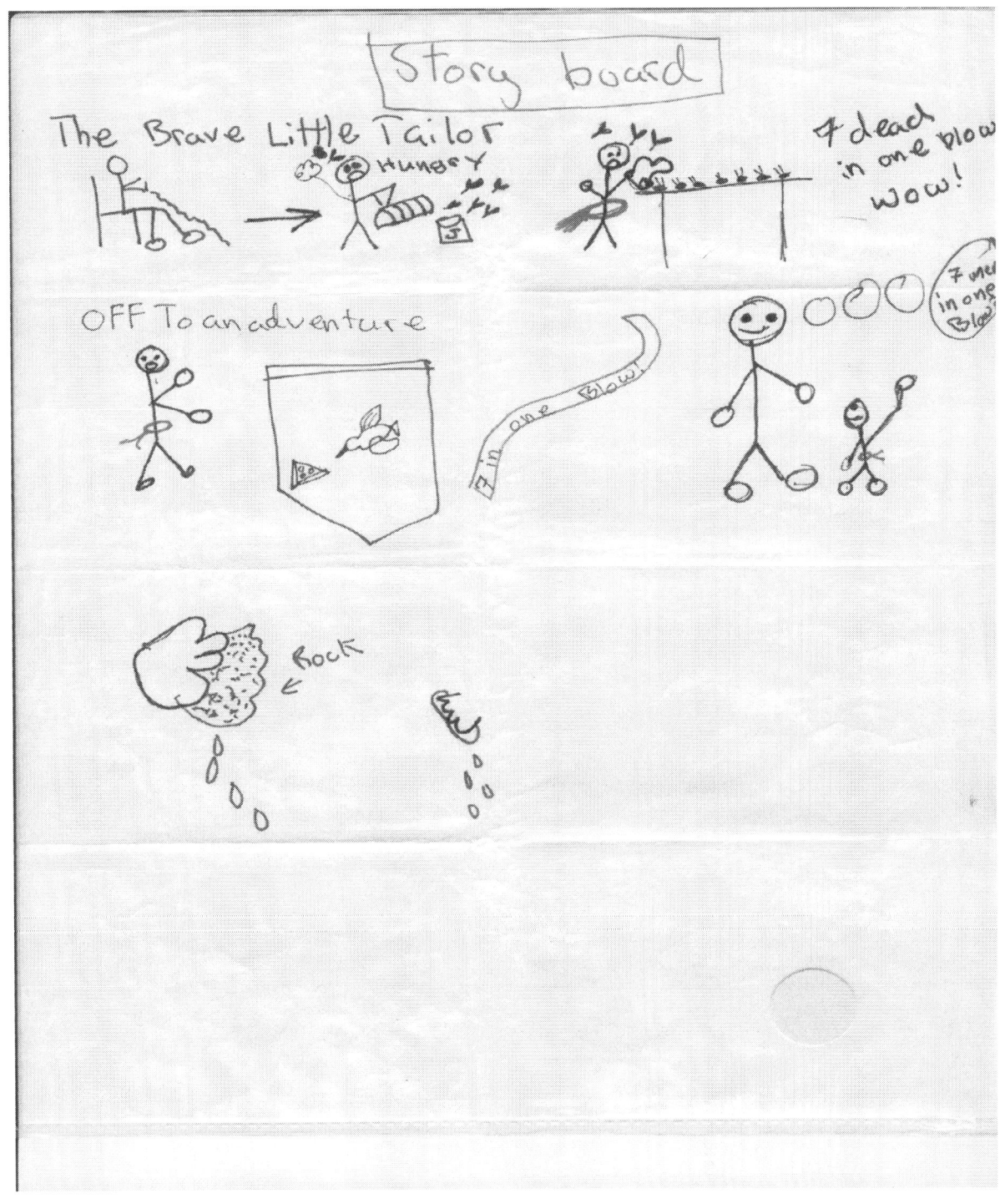

If you don't have cash register or adding machine tape, you might use copy paper folded into sections to form a sequential story board.

Assessment:

Sequencing Rubric:

CATEGORY	1	2	3	4
Neatness and Presentation	Is not neat enough to understand.	Well-presented with some of the information is difficult to understand.	Most of the information is easy to understand.	All the information is easy to understand
Use of images/symbols	The sequence strip includes some images.	A few labels are enhanced with simple symbols or diagrams	Some labels are enhanced with simple symbols or diagrams	Most labels are enhanced with simple symbols or diagrams
Use of color	The sequence strip lacks color.	The color used does not categorize or chunk information.	Color is used to demonstrate some connections and or topics throughout the sequence strip	Color is used show all connections and/or to categorize topics throughout the sequence strip
Includes major events	Many major events are excluded, and too many trivial events are included.	Some events included are trivial, and major events are missing.	Most of the included events are important or interesting; one or two major events.	Included events are important and interesting; no major details are excluded.

Group & Classify Information to Enhance Long-term Memory

Background:
Graphic organizers compliment the way the brain naturally categorizes information. The schema, or mental structure, of the mind contains all of our preexisting knowledge sorted into themes. As the mind takes in new information, it matches it with an already familiar theme in order to make sense of it. The use of mind-maps in the classroom provides students with a visual way to categorize data which will in turn make new information easier for students to comprehend. It also increases their ability to recall the information at a later date. (Ausubel, 1963; Hyerle, 2009; Marzano, Pickering, Pollock, et al., 2001; Moore, 1984)

Learning objectives:
- Organize information according to a theme
- Discover how sub-themes are interrelated.
- Analyze information and summarize it leaving out extraneous information.
- Use appropriate vocabulary in describing the features observed.

Application to Response to Intervention Tiers:

TIER ONE	TIER TWO	TIER THREE
Teacher uses strategy with entire class to differentiate instruction	Place students in preselected small groups to enable a specialist to support them through the process using targeted questioning techniques that encourage understanding of categorization. As often as possible, incorporate categorization activities in student learning.	Student works with a specialist one-to-one for an additional 60 to 90 minutes per week using this intervention as a strategy to facilitate comprehension ability to categorize.

Addresses the following non-responder indicators
- Auditory learning deficit
- Note taking deficiencies
- Attention deficit disorder
- Difficulty connecting to connect new information with previously learned knowledge
- Difficulty activating prior knowledge; difficulty retrieving information learned
- Difficulty remembering what the teacher says in class
- Difficulty recoding incoming information into meaningful information
- Difficulty with higher order thinking such as problem solving and comparing and contrasting

Materials needed:
- Literature: books of various genres
- Genre information
- Rubric
- Group segment of the mind map and blank individual mind maps(For a sample mind map, see Figure 16 Sample Classification Mind Map from Inspiration.com)
- Colored pencils/pens/markers for each group

Approximate time frame for completion:
- Main Lesson - one class period
- Extension Learning - Variable

Intervention Procedure & Scripts:

Part One, Tier One/Whole Group

Discuss the theme of genre with the students.

Draw a mind map on the board and write the word genre along with its definition in the middle of it. Genre is a literary composition characterized by its style, form, or content.

Examples of genre are allegory, comedy, creative nonfiction, epic, essay, lyric, motion picture scenario, novel, pastoral, satire, short story, television play, tragedy, poetry, science fiction, fantasy, fairy tales, tall tales, folk tales, myths and legends, historical fiction, mystery, non-fiction, biography, and autobiography.

Part Two, Tier One/Tier Two/Small Groups

1. Place students in preselected small groups (3-5 students), insuring a mixture of ability levels.
2. Hand out an assortment of books, children's books representing a variety of reading levels and sophistication, or short stories to each small group.
3. Ask students to look through their group's books and use a list of genres to classify the books.
4. <u>They may create their own classifications or include some not on the list.</u> The key to having them create their own is whether they can explain the rationale behind the genre.

Part Three, Tier One/Whole Group

4. Once they have compiled a list, discuss each group's findings as a class.
5. Guide a discussion and have each group share a genre they identified and record it on the board. Continue until a good amount of genres have been identified and listed.

6. Choose one genre as an example and create extensions of that section of the mind-map. Add literary examples of that classification with the class.
7. Use a different color for each section to help students visualize the classifications.

Part Four, Tier One/Tier Two/Small Groups

6. Have students return to their groups

7. Each group will become an expert on a particular genre.

8. Set a specific amount of time for students to acquire their expertise and be ready to report out.

   a. Each group must read the information provided for their assigned genre.
   b. Complete their mind-map using different colors for each section (group, examples, characteristic, and implications).
   c. Write the name of their genre on their mind-map
   d. Provide two examples of books in their assigned genre. They may use books from the previous exercise for ideas.
   e. Determine three characteristics which best set their genre apart from the others. (Some characteristics are more generic and could apply to multiple genres).
   f. Add the genres to their mind-map, in the characteristic boxes.
   g. Determine the implications of each of the three characteristics they identified
   h. Write them down in the boxes provided.
   i. Create visuals to support the concepts in their mind map.
   j. Use least three illustrations that represent their assigned genre.
      a. For example, if they were assigned Mystery, they might draw a question mark, a magnifying class, and a detective.

Teacher:
- Hand out one segment of the mind map, genre information, game card sheet, box of colored pencils, and rubrics to each group.
- Rotate around the room and provide support as needed.

Part Five, Tier One/Whole Group

1. Give each student a blank mind-map to fill in as each group presents their genre.
2. After each group presents their mind maps to the class have the group attach their contribution to the class mind-map. (You will have a complete mind-map representing all of the genres once all of the groups are finished presenting.)

Extension:
Students may compare and contrast two similar genres using the genre comparison sheet. (See Figure 17 Compare & Contrast Genre Map) For example: science fiction and fantasy,

myths and legends and tall tales, biography and autobiography, and fairy tales and folk tales .

To differentiate:
- Place students in mixed-ability groups.
- Students with difficulty in note taking will be provided with a typed copy of the mind map once it is complete.
- The students will choose their own literature which will have a wide range of reading levels.

Across the Curriculum:
Mind-maps can be used when you want to cover a large amount of material quickly. After you have introduced the initial theme, groups can each be given a piece of the unit to research and use a mind-map to record their information. As each group presents their information to the class, the others will add the information to their mind-maps.

A mind-map can also be used to introduce a new unit or theme and then be added to as new information or definitions are introduced to the class. Each student should be given a blank copy of the mind-map which they can fill in so they have their own copy to study from. This provides a great way to review daily and connect all the material in a logical way. Students can then use their mind-maps to study before a test. Mind maps are more efficient than traditional notes because when students study they are able to see the whole concept and how everything connects. Mind maps also teach to a variety of learning preferences at the same time.

- Social Studies teachers can use this approach to organize a specific theme as it applies to different time periods or social groups. For example: technology and its effects on the family unit, the doctrine of non-violence and how it has influenced social change, transportation and how it has encouraged globalization.
- Science teachers can use this strategy to connect new definitions to a central theme as they are introduced. For example, the periodic table and the element groups/families, habitats and their characteristics, or the human body and its systems.
- Math teachers might apply this to areas such as geometry and proofs, algebra and types of equations, or trigonometry and angles.
- In all subject areas, teachers may apply classification and grouping in a variety of ways other than that presented
    - For independent writing assignments, have students write a short story, play, or short comic book that applies to the area of study.
    - For independent reading, students select books or articles on the subject area and build a mind map covering the characteristics being studied.

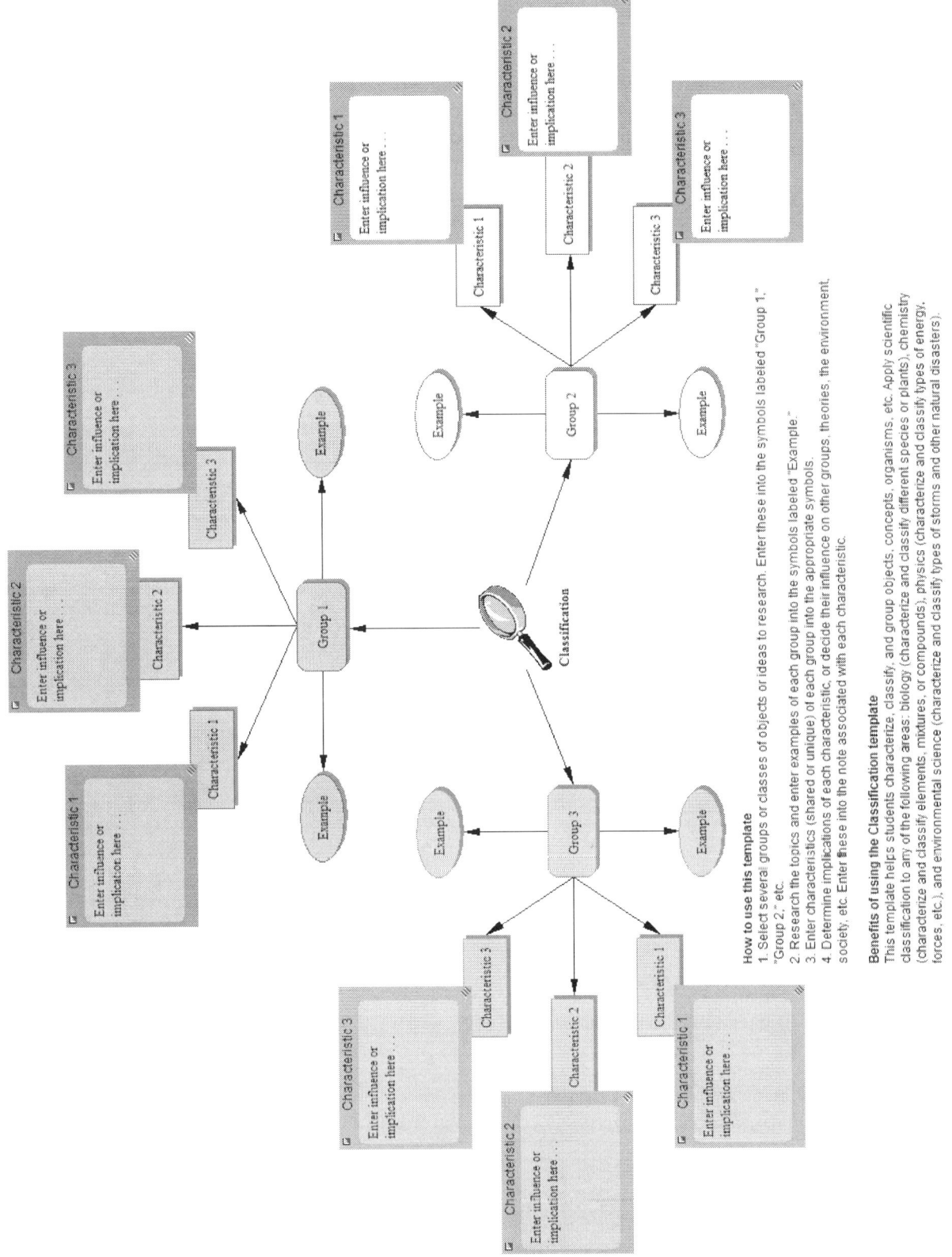

Figure 16 Sample Classification Mind Map from Inspiration.com

Extension:

Compare & Contrast Genre Map

Directions: Choose two similar genres and compare and contrast them.

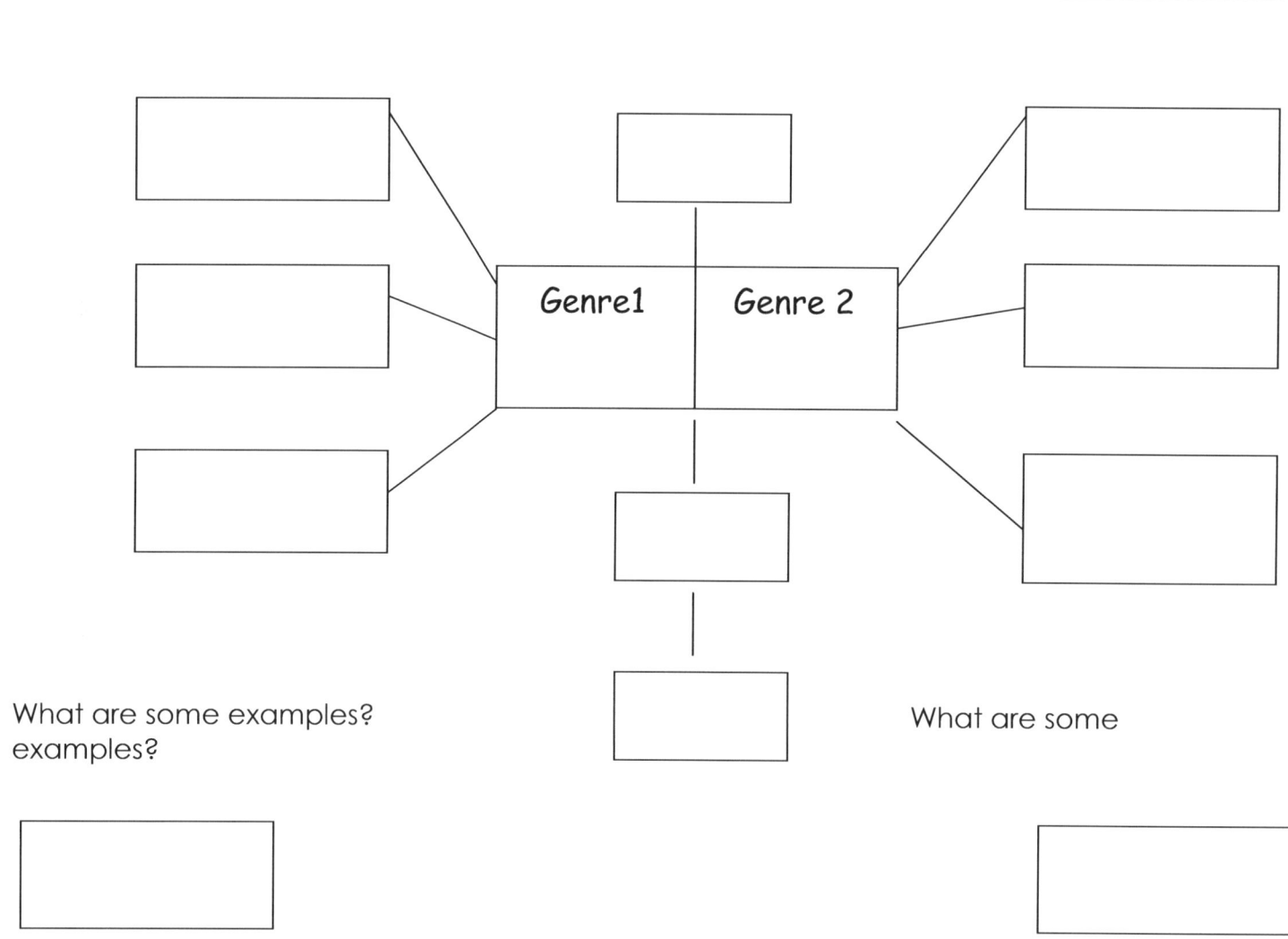

What are some examples?
examples?

What are some

Figure 17 Compare & Contrast Genre Map

Assessment:

Mind Map Rubric

CATEGORY	1	2	3	4
Neatness and Presentation	Portions are illegible. Genre-related words are misspelled. Multiple sections are written all in one color.	The presentation is messy. Three to four genre-related words are misspelled. Each section is written in a different color.	The presentation appears neat and orderly overall. Genre-related words are spelled correctly.	The presentation is exceptionally neat and orderly.
Use of images/symbols	None of the pictures are accurate symbols of the assigned genre.	Three of the five pictures are accurate symbols of the assigned genre.	Four of the five pictures are accurate symbols of the assigned genre.	All the pictures drawn are accurate symbols of the assigned genre.
Use of art	Pictures are not completed.	Coloring lacks sufficient detail and has a rushed appearance.	Colored pictures lack sufficient detail, but do enhance the overall look of the mind map	Five neatly colored and accurate pictures enhance the overall look of the mind map.
Understanding	The mind map is not filled in correctly. The implications developed are illogical or incomplete.	The mind map is filled in correctly overall. Most of the implications developed are logical.	The mind map is filled in correctly. The student developed fairly logical implications for each of the three genre characteristics.	The mind map is filled in correctly. The student developed strong logical implications for each of the three genre characteristics.

Analogies

Background

When people use analogies to learn a new topic or solve a problem, they have a higher success rate because they make connections between new knowledge and familiar ideas or models (schema). When three groups of people were asked to solve a medical problem, 75% of the group that was told to use an analogy to solve the problem was successful (Gick, 1983). Analogies prove to be a useful tool in the classroom. Rule and Furletti (Rule, 2004), found that form and analogy boxes improved student performance when learning about different body systems. Analogy boxes contain objects and cards that demonstrate similarities between the new concept (*i.e.* the eye of the nervous system) and the analogy (a camera lens).

Students will enjoy higher levels of success when they are very familiar with the analogies used. In a study by Friedel, Gabel, & Samuel in 1990,(Friedel, 1990) teachers often used analogies that related to their own experience and, as a result, students failed to understand the relationships between the new concept and analogy (as cited in Rule and Furletti, 2004). Teachers must choose analogies that their students will understand as well as emphasize the limits of the analogy to prevent student misconception.

Learning objectives:
- enhance long-term memory: recall & recognition
- make connections between the known and unknown
- increase comprehension by relating the known with the unknown

Application to Response to Intervention Tiers:

TIER ONE	TIER TWO	TIER THREE
Students brainstorm one or more possible contemporary analogies for abstract concepts as needed to create connections and enhance understanding.	Provide a specific analogy and guide student(s) through the process of brainstorming connections between the new concept and the analogy. *Repeat practice until student can apply skill independently.*	A specialist provides a specific analogy and guides student through the process of brainstorming connections between the new concept and the analogy. Break the process into steps. Repeat practice until student can apply skill independently. Provide time every day to make connections to content through analogies.

Addresses the following non-responder indicators:
- Long-term memory deficits
- Comprehension of new and abstract concepts
- Difficulty relating and/or applying new information
- Difficulty processing information in a way that is meaningful to them.
- Unable to connect new information with previously learned knowledge
- Does not activate prior knowledge; difficulty retrieving information learned
- Trouble remembering what the teacher says in class
- Difficulty retaining information
- Unable to recode incoming information into meaningful information
- Automaticity of skill development

Materials needed:

A description of the new concept you are about to teach. It might be process such as how a Bill becomes a Law, or an historical event such as The Cold War (See

Figure 18 Mind Map Example: Cold War), The French Revolution, or a person such as the President of the United States. Students should have read the description before beginning the lesson.

Approximate time frame for completion:
- Brainstorming the analogy - 10-20 minutes
- Resulting discussion and creating visual/written representations of analogy – variable

Intervention Procedure & Scripts:
Tier One/Whole Class

1. Either in small groups or at the board, students generate a list of adjectives or steps to describe the event, process, or person at the center of the lesson.
2. Students brainstorm one or more possible contemporary analogies for the event or person. For example, students might compare The Cold War to a tumultuous teenage relationship, the President of the United States to the school's principal, or how a Bill becomes a Law to a person on a trip with different stops along the way.

Tier One or Tier Two/ Whole class, small group or individualized

3. Students then create visual representations of their analogies.
   a. Students can create a Venn diagram (See Figure 19 Venn Diagram Example) to find basic similarities and differences between concept and analog.
   b. Students can create a mind map to connect the new concept with analogy.

c. Students can create written memory models in which they elaborate on the similarities and differences involved.

d. Student find physical object that can be used as an analogy.

To differentiate:
- Ask higher level students to brainstorm an original analog and its resulting connections.
- Provide a specific analogy to lower level students and ask them to brainstorm connections between the new concept and the analogy.

Application Example:
Social Studies: Read short bio article on the current United States President (http://www.whitehouse.gov/about/presidents).

1. List 5-8 characteristics of the President. (*i.e.* ambitious, won election to become president, helps develop laws).

2. Create list of 5-8 characteristics of the person being compared (Principal, Parent, etc.).

3. Create a Venn diagram to show similarities and differences between the two people.

Across the Curriculum:
Science teachers can use analogies to help students understand the system of the body. Some examples:

		Flap inside = epiglottis Filter = cilia Canister = lung	Mini-maze = Alveoli (demonstrating the exchange of O_2 and CO_2)
Diagram used to teach the respiratory system	Corrugated hose = trachea Ribbing in hose = cartilage	Sponge = Lung tissue	Line up 'models' in the order they would be in the respiratory system.

The Circulatory System is like the Mail Delivery System

- Arteries – Highways that the postal truck travels
- Veins – Neighborhood Streets
- Parts of the body nutrients delivered to – Houses mail delivered to
- Blood Cell – Postal Truck
- Nutrients – Mail
- Waste (Carbon Dioxide) – Junk mail/garbage

Authentic Assessment:

English/Language Arts: Students write a paragraph to explain how a new concept is similar to an analogy they have generated.

1. Include and explain at least three similarities
2. Include one to two limitations of the analogy, *i.e.*, how the concept is unlike the analogy.

Rubric: Connect Similarities and Differences between New Concept and Analog

CATEGORY	1	2	3	4
Identify similarities and differences between new concept and analog.	Does not make connections between new concept and analog.	Distinguishes general similarities and differences between concept and analog.	Elaborates on similarities and differences between concept and analog.	Creates new analogs for the concept.

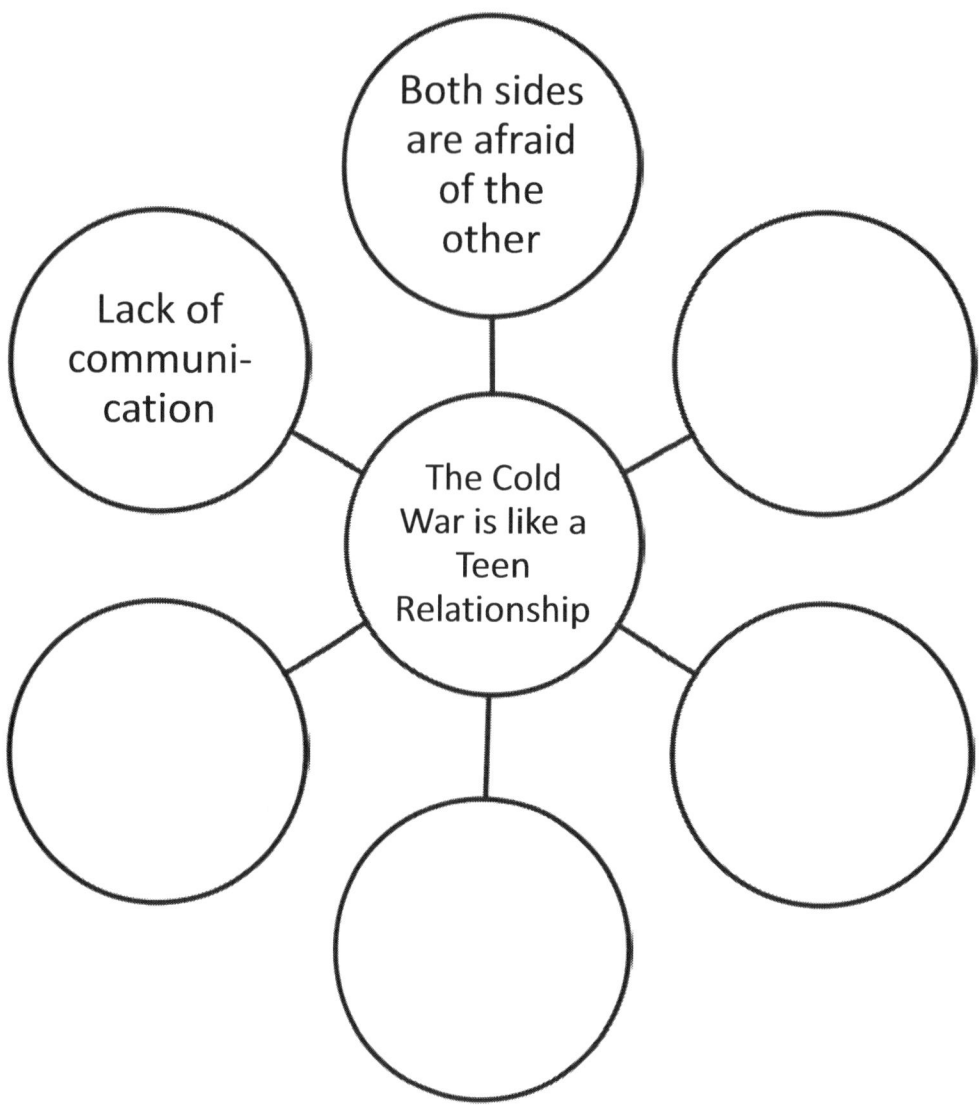

Figure 18 Mind Map Example: Cold War

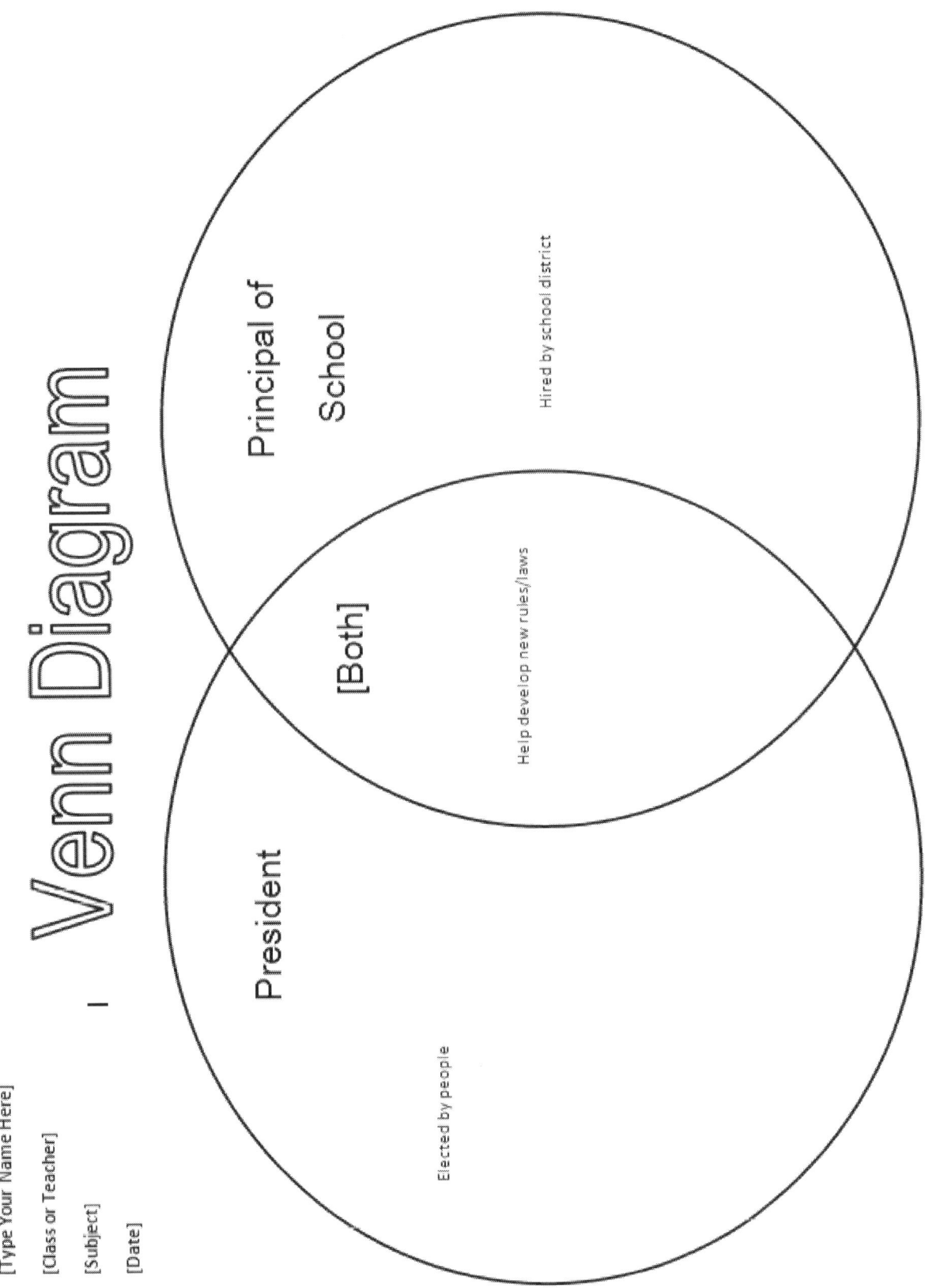

Venn Diagram

[Type Your Name Here]

[Class or Teacher]

[Subject]

[Date]

President

Principal of School

[Both]

Elected by people

Help develop new rules/laws

Hired by school district

Figure 19 Venn Diagram Example

Teaching Summarizing Skills

Background
Summarizing is a life-long skill that greatly impacts student learning. When students learn to effectively summarize, their comprehension, their ability to identify key information and retain information improves.(Anderson & Armbruster;Denner;Einstein, 1986; 1986; 1985; Laboratory, 2005)

Learning Objective:
- Identify the main ideas in various types of writing.
- Create topic sentences to present an overall summary of a piece of writing.
- Apply a specific summarization strategy (Delete-Substitute-Keep) to various types of writing.
- Synthesize information and present it in a way that is meaningful to them.
- Enhance their comprehension through summarization.
- Apply summarization strategies in many curricular areas.
- Recognize the importance of summarization in "real world" applications.

Application to Response to Intervention Tiers:

TIER ONE	TIER TWO	TIER THREE
Teacher uses strategy with entire class to differentiate instruction	Student(s) use summarizing strategy as they proceed with assigned reading. Student works with a peer tutor, specialist or in a coaching session with the classroom teacher at least twice per week until the study strategy is internalized.	Student works with a specialist one-to-one for an additional 60-90 minutes per week using The independent practice protocol as an intervention to facilitate summarization skills.

Addresses the following non-responder indicators:
- Struggle to effectively use words to express organized and complete thoughts in writing
- Reading difficulties
- Processing disorders
- Word usage skills below standard
- Difficulty linking prior knowledge to new information
- Poor memory
- Difficulty processing information in a way that is meaningful to them
- Difficulty organizing information
- note taking deficiencies

Materials needed:

- Literature (magazine or newspaper articles, textbooks, poetry, novels, short stories, non-fiction and fiction texts, websites, blogs)
- A soft ball or Koosh Ball

Approximate time frame for completion:

- Story retell – 5-10 minutes
- Direct instruction – 15-20 minutes (variable depending on article length and student participation)
- Jigsaw – 20 minutes (variable depending on article length and student understanding)
- Independent Practice – 20-30 minutes (variable depending on article length and student understanding)

Intervention procedure & scripts:

Tier One/Whole Class

Story Retell

A quick, easy way to introduce summarization is to do a story retell. This strategy helps students to identify main ideas. You can use it with a story that the class recently read, a movie, or something as basic as a fairy tale. You could even use it to review a class lesson. The key is to choose something with which all students are familiar so that everyone can participate in a whole class environment.

a) Have the students stand in a circle. Give one student a soft ball (Koosh or Nerf).
b) The student holding the ball begins to retell the story with one beginning sentence. He then throws the ball to another student.
c) The next student tells another important event in the story and throws the ball to another student.
d) The students continue to pass the ball and tell a story event until they get to the end of the story.

Tier One/Whole Class

Delete-Substitute-Keep Strategy(Brown, 1981)

a) Place a sample article on an overhead projector (computer, etc.) so all students can see.
b) Read the article aloud and then have students reread the article silently.
c) Turn off the projector and ask students to provide one sentence to summarize the article. List all possible suggestions on the board.
d) Turn the projector back on and have students give suggestions for what unnecessary words or sentences to DELETE. Do the same thing for redundant sentences. (Do this in red)

e) Go through the article and SUBSTITUTE super-ordinate terms. For example, "trees" for pines, oaks and maples (Do this in blue).
f) Reread the article without all of the deleted items. Refer back to the one sentence summaries and choose the TOPIC SENTENCE that fits best.
g) Write the summary beginning with the topic sentence. Cover the article and have students provide key ideas in their own words. When they get stuck, or think they are finished, they may refer back to the article to ensure they have included all of the necessary information and to check for accuracy.

Tier Two/Small Group:

Delete-Substitute-Keep Strategy is an excellent partner activity as well as a student/specialist intervention activity.

Tier One/Small Group

Jigsaw

The Jigsaw Strategy (Aronson & Patnoe, 1997) is a great way to help students practice summarization skills. Each student (or group) is assigned a section of an article, chapter, or book (the whole puzzle). They are responsible for reading that section (their piece) and teaching the rest of the class about their part. By teaching it to others they will have to clearly convey the main ideas of their reading to ensure that all students understand all pieces of the puzzle.

- Place students in mixed ability groups
- Assign each group a section of the reading
- Students thoroughly read their assigned piece
- Students apply the summarization strategies modeled by the teacher (above)
- Students report their summaries to the remainder of the class

If students do this correctly, they will have a complete understanding of the entire reading, even though they did not read the entire piece themselves. They will love not having to read the entire passage and thus will be motivated to do a good job!

(See application example for optional suggestions)

Tier Two/Tier Three: Independent Practice

Blind Summarizing:

1. Read the article twice.
2. *Cover up the article and summarize it in one sentence.*
3. Delete unnecessary words, sentences, and redundancies.
4. Substitute super-ordinate terms (for example, "trees" for pines, oaks and maples)
5. Reread the article without all of the deleted items. Refine the TOPIC SENTENCE
6. Write the summary beginning with the topic sentence. Cover the article and add main ideas in your own words. Refer back to the article for ideas and to check for accuracy.

Optional Supports:

1. Create a small cue cardFigure 20 Steps to Summarizing Cue Card) that students can keep on their desk or in their folder to remind them of these steps:
   - Delete unnecessary words or sentences
   - Delete redundant words or sentences
   - Substitute super-ordinate terms (for example, "trees" for pines, oaks, and maples)
   - Select or create a topic sentence
2. If photocopies are unavailable, provide students with highlighting tape to write on or use of an overhead transparency to lay over the text.
3. Students can use pre-selected articles or choose their own articles. If they are choosing their own articles help them to pick materials at their appropriate reading level in order to provide an appropriate challenge while avoiding frustration.
4. You may want to provide students with a checklist for their summary writing. (See Figure 21 Check Your Summary Cue Card
   - Does your topic sentence synthesize all important information?
   - Are the main ideas clear and accurate?
   - Is your summary concise?
   - Does your summary maintain the author's voice?
   - Did you leave out unnecessary words and sentences?
   - Did you replace super-ordinate terms?

Application example:
This example illustrates the jigsaw technique. While the literature example is intended for educators, it clearly demonstrates that this technique can be adapted to any type of literature, text book chapter, or lengthy article.

Reflection Notes

1. Divide the class into five equal groups. (This varies depending on the amount of material)
    Assign each group a section to read in chapter 3 of the book, *Classroom Instruction that Works* by Marzano, Pickering, and Pollock.

    - Group A: "Research and Theory on Summarizing" p.30-32
    - Group B: "Classroom Practice in Summarizing" p. 32-34
    - Group C: "Summary Frames" p.34-37
    - Group D: "Summary Frames" p.37-42
    - Group E: "Reciprocal Teaching" p42-43

2. Each group reads their selection and then applies the "Delete-Substitute-Keep" strategy in order to prepare their summary.
3. Each group presents their summary to the rest of the class (in the same order that the text is presented).

To differentiate:
Depending on the material, groups can be arranged in different ways.

- If the material is fairly consistent, use mixed ability groups.
- If there are more difficult concepts integrated with basic concepts, groups can be more homogeneous and the sections given to each group can be catered to individual ability levels.
- If it is a longer section (for example an entire book) you can create dyads in order to cover more material.
- Students can be divided into groups and each person can be responsible for a jigsaw section in order to individualize the practice.

Across the Curriculum:
This strategy can be applied to all curriculum areas. Here are some examples:
- In Social Studies, it can be used to preview an entire

chapter. Each group can "become the expert" on a particular section of the chapter (or even the entire book depending on your purpose).

- In Science, each group can present a different research study about a particular concept.
- In Math, students can read about different strategies to solving the same type of problem.
- In Physical Education students can read and present about different techniques to achieve optimal health.

As long as there is something to read, students can practice these summarizing strategies!

For Independent Writing Assignments:
The Delete-Substitute-Keep strategy most directly lends itself to individual writing assignments in which students are using literary resources to obtain information. However, the retelling strategy can also be used - just have the student write down their retell! Students can also write down their individual portion of a jigsaw.

For Independent Reading Assignments (literature or content area):
All three strategies (retelling, jigsaw, delete-substitute-keep) can be applied to independent reading assignments.

For Group Brainstorming and Mind Map Creation:
All three summarizing strategies can be applied to group brainstorming and mind mapping. Students can help one another to understand the process and further develop their skills.

Extension:
Students may select their own articles in order to find material that meets their interest and academic ability level. They may even seek out interesting pieces that they would like the class to jigsaw.

Assessment:

Rubric: Summarizing Pieces of Literature

CATEGORY	1	2	3	4
Topic Sentence	Topic sentence focuses on details and does not summarize.	Generally states the big ideas in the literature but does not narrow it to one overall topic sentence.	Identifies the main idea but does not synthesize all of the necessary information.	Succinctly hones in on the main idea with a topic sentence that synthesizes all of the relevant information, creating an umbrella for the rest of the paragraph.
Main Ideas	Does not discern main ideas from the details.	Picks out big ideas but includes some details.	Identifies the main ideas.	Identifies and synthesizes the main ideas.
Deleting/ Substituting	Does not differentiate between necessary and unnecessary information and lacks substitute words; struggles to find words to substitute.	Deletes and substitutes some of the unnecessary and redundant information, but struggles to substitute with more general terms.	Deletes and substitutes unnecessary and redundant information.	Creatively deletes and substitutes all unnecessary and redundant information from the literature while maintaining the integrity of the author's writing..

Draw it so that you'll know it![8]

Reflection Notes

Condense information into a picture and embrace the power of color. Teachers often present information verbally and linguistically. However, many of our students are visual learners. A substantial amount of our brain power is devoted to visual processing. When teachers add a visual component, a drawing component, to what they are teaching, student recall increases(Aronson & Patnoe, 1997; Ewy, 2003; Hyerle, 2009; Pehrsson & Denner, 1989).

For example, after teaching for five or six minutes at the elementary level, or up to ten minutes in a high school class, give students three to five minutes to draw a picture, diagram, or symbol of what they just learned. This strategy lets students take the verbal linguistic information we just taught and turn it into visual information. This lets the brain process and use information in a different way which, in turn, helps students to better remember what has been taught.

When we use drawing exercises in the classroom, we often encounter resistance from students. They complain that they can't draw. One way to address this is to draw badly when we draw in the classroom. Use stick figure drawings and emphasize the importance of simple line drawings over drawing well. The point is to create an image that helps us remember what we've learned, not to get graded on our art.

If students say they can't draw, pair them up with someone who doesn't mind drawing. It would be a shame to lose students because of their initial resistance to doing something so different from what they are used to doing in school.

The brain has a huge capacity for visual processing, so the visual component of our memory is very powerful.

Snapshot Devices

Another way to present information visually is to use a snapshot device. Snapshot devices take the concepts we've already talked about to another level because their purpose is to take a 'snapshot' of information and represent it visually so students will remember it. For instance, you've taught about how the West

---

[8] Memorization and Test Taking Strategies for the Differentiated, Inclusive and RTI Classroom by Susan Gingras Fitzell, Cogent Catalyst Publications, 2010

was settled and explained that certain inventions were involved, such as the six-shooter, the windmill, the sod house, the locomotive, and barbed wire.

A snapshot device is a picture with all of the things you've taught in it. However, it's a scene, not just a collection of individual pictures. If you just draw pictures of a six-shooter, a windmill, and a sod house, with no way to relate these things to each other, you are drawing 'unconnected' images. With a snapshot device, you take the information and make it into a scene to think about. Students will remember the cowboy with the six-shooters and the train coming down the hill behind the sod house. They will see the scene in their mind's eye.

Assessing with Visuals
When students are engaged in drawing what they've learned, teachers have an opportunity to walk around the room and assess understanding by looking at students' drawings and asking questions for clarification. Document your observations and you'll have a form of authentic and immediate ongoing assessment.

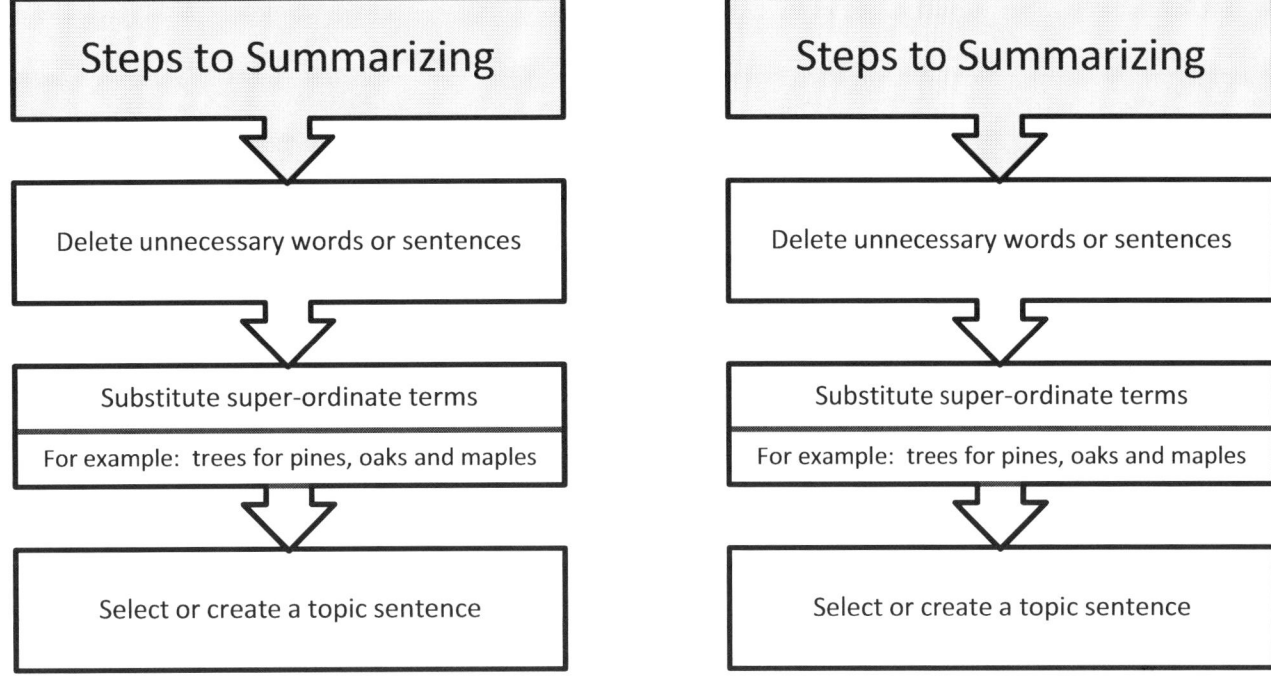

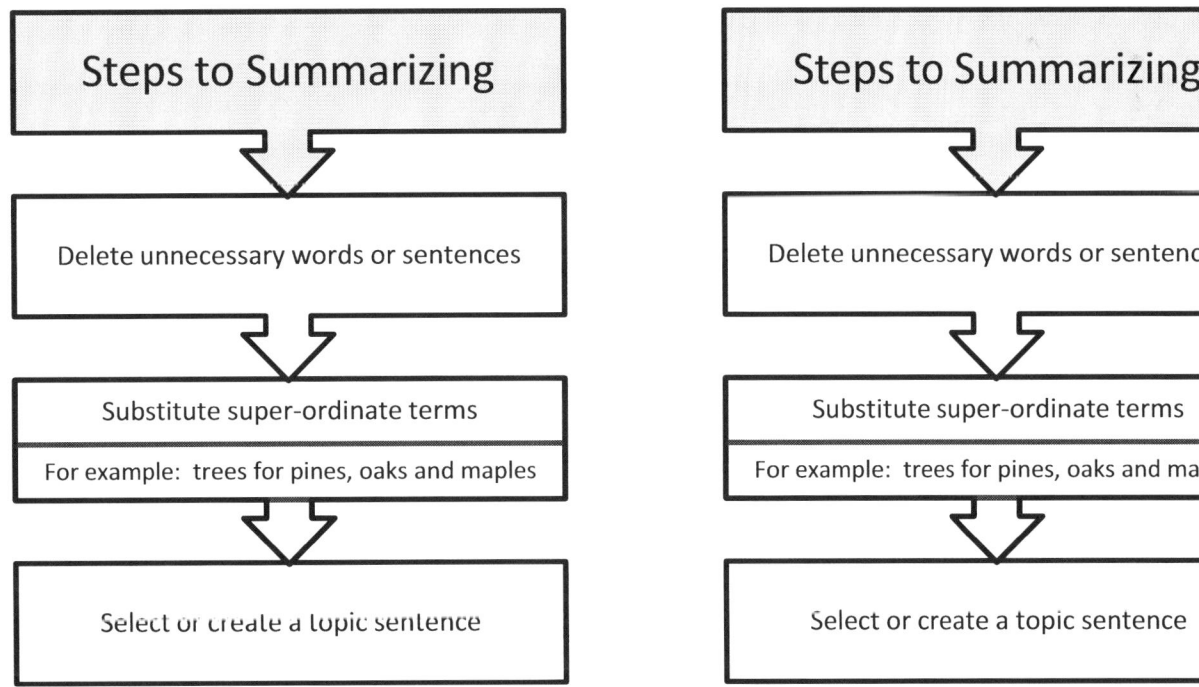

Figure 20 Steps to Summarizing Cue Card

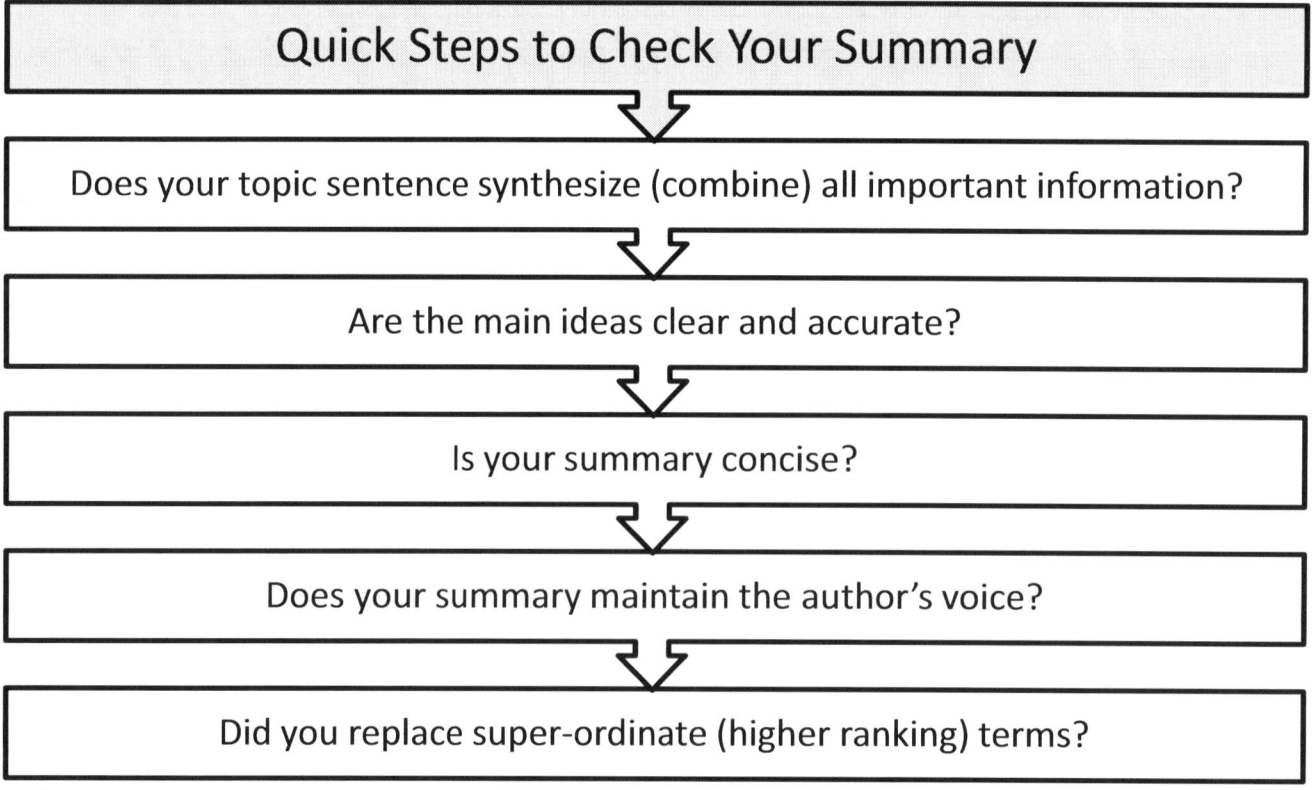

Quick Steps to Check Your Summary

Does your topic sentence synthesize (combine) all important information?

Are the main ideas clear and accurate?

Is your summary concise?

Does your summary maintain the author's voice?

Did you replace super-ordinate (higher ranking) terms?

Quick Steps to Check Your Summary

Does your topic sentence synthesize (combine) all important information?

Are the main ideas clear and accurate?

Is your summary concise?

Does your summary maintain the author's voice?

Did you replace super-ordinate (higher ranking) terms?

Figure 21 Check Your Summary Cue Card

Bibliography

Anderson & Armbruster;Denner;Einstein, M., & Smith. (1986; 1986; 1985). When students review and revise their own notes, the notes become more meaningful and useful

Aronson, E., & Patnoe, S. (1997). *The jigsaw classroom : building cooperation in the classroom* (2nd ed.). New York: Longman.

Ausubel, D. P. (1963). *The Psychology of Meaningful Verbal Learning: An introduction to school learning*. New York: Grune & Statton.

Bender, W., & Shores, C. (2007). *Response to Intervention a Practical Guide for Every Teacher*. Thousand Oaks, California: Corwin Press.

Bickmore, S. B., Jacqueline; Hundley, Melanie;. (2001). Picture Books for Young Adult Readers. *The Alan Review, 28*(3).

Brown-Chidsey, R., & Steege, M. W. (2005). *Response to Intervention Principles And Strategies for Effective Practice*. New York, NY: The Guilford Press.

Brown, C., & Day. (1981). Teach a formal process. Teach students the delete-substitute-keep process for summarizing. A "rule-based strategy" for summarizing includes a specific set of steps.

Ewy, C. A. (2003). *Teaching with visual frameworks : focused learning and achievement through instructional graphics co-created by students and teachers*. Thousand Oaks, Calif: Corwin Press.

Fox, D. L., & Short, K. G. (2003). *Stories matter : the complexity of cultural authenticity in children's literature*. Urbana, Ill.: National Council of Teachers of English.

Friedel, A. W., Gabel, D.I., & Samuel, J. (1990). Using analogs for chemistry problem solving: Does it increase understanding? . *School Science and Mathematics, 90*, 674-682.

Gick, M. H., Kieth. (1983). Schema Induction & Analogical Transfer. *Cognitivce Psych, Vol. 15*, 138.

Hadaway, N. L., & Mundy, J. (1999). Children's Informational Picture Books Visit a Secondary ESL Classroom. *Journal of Adolescent & Adult Literacy Vol. 42*(6,), 464-476.

Hall, S. L. (2008). *Implementing Response to Intervention: A Principal's Guide*. Thousands Oaks, California: Corwin Press.

Hanson, H. M. (2009). *RTI and DI: Response to Intervention and Differentiated Instruction*.

Harvey, S. G., Anne. (2007). *Strategies that work: teaching comprehension for understanding and engagement*: Stenhouse Publishers, Penbroke Publishers Limited.

Hyerle, D. (2009). *Visual tools for transforming information into knowledge* (2nd ed.). Thousand Oaks, CA: Corwin Press.

James, I. T. S. C. (2007). Questioning and informational texts: scaffolding students comprehension of content areas. *Forum on Public Policy: A Journal of the Oxford Round Table. Forum on Public Policy*.

Johnson Nancy J., G. C. (Ed.). (2007). *The Wonder of It All When Literature and Literacy Intersect*: Heinemann.

Koehler, L. J. S. L., Lyle L. (1986). *Using Fingerspelling/Manual Signs to Facilitate Reading and Spelling*. Paper presented at the Biennial Conference of the International Society for Augmentative and Alternative Communication.

Laboratory, N. R. E. (2005). Summarizing and Note Taking. Retrieved 3 February, 2010, from netc.org/focus/strategies/summ.php

Lederer, J. M. (2000). Reciprocal Teaching of Social Studies in Inclusive Elementary Classrooms. *Journal of Learning Disabilities. Sage Publications, Inc.*

Levine, D. M. (2003). *A Mind At A Time.* New York, NY: Simon and Schuster.

Marzano, R. J., & Mid-continent Regional Educational Laboratory. (1991). *Literacy plus. An integrated approach to teaching reading, writing, vocabulary, and reasoning, teacher guide.* Columbus, Ohio: Zaner-Bloser, Inc.

Marzano, R. J., Pickering, D., Pollock, J. E., & ebrary Inc. (2001). Classroom instruction that works research-based strategies for increasing student achievementpp. vi, 187 p.).

Marzano, R. J., Pickering, D. J., & Pollock, J. E. (2001). *Classroom Instruction That Works: research-based strategies for increasing student achievement.* Alexandria, VA: Association for Supervision and Curriculum Development.

Miller, G. A. The Magical Number Seven, Plus or Minus Two: Some Limits on Our Capacity for Processing Information. *The Psychological Review, 63,* 81-97.

Moore, D. W., & Readence, J. E. . (1984). A quantitative and qualitative review of graphic organizer research. Journal of Educational Research. 78, 11- 17.

National Reading Panel. (2000). *Teaching children to read: An evidence-based assessment of the scientific research literature on reading and its implications for reading instruction.* (Report). Washington, DC: National Institute of Child Health and Human Development.

O'Donnell, A. M., & King, A. (1999). *Cognitive perspectives on peer learning.* Mahwah, N.J.: L. Erlbaum.

Palincsar, A. S. L. R. H. (2002). Designing collaborative learning contexts. *Theory into Practice, The Ohio State University, on behalf of its College of Education.*

Pehrsson, R. S., & Denner, P. R. (1989). *Semantic organizers : a study strategy for special needs learners.* Rockville, MD: Aspen Publishers.

Picciotto, H. (2010). Algebra Manipulatives: Comparison and History Retrieved from http://www.MathEdPage.org/manipulatives/alg-manip.html

Raskinski, T. V. (2003). *The Fluent reader* (Imported edition ed.). New York: Teaching Resources

Reys, R. E., Lambdin, D. V., Lindquist, M., & Smith, N. L. (2009). *Helping children learn mathematics, 9th Edition* (2nd ed.). Englewood Cliffs, N.J.: Prentice Hall.

Robinson, B. (2007, April 10, 2007). *Using Picture Books to Teach Literary Terms in the High School English Classroom,* University of North Carolina - Ashville.

Rule, A. C. F., Charles. (2004). Using form and function analogy object boxes to teach human body systems. *School Science and Mathematics.*

Shores, C., & Chester, K. (2009). *Using RTI for School Improvement: Raising Every Student Achievement Scores.* Thousand Oaks, California: Corwin Press.

Shugarman, S. L. H., Joe B. (1986). Purposeful Paraphrasing: Promoting a Nontrivial Pursuit for Meaning. *Journal of Reading, 29*(5), 396-399.

Wright, J. (2007). *RTI Toolkit a Practical Guide for Schools.* Port Chester, NY: Dude Publishing.

Index

Bright Ideas

Bright Ideas

Your Gift for Attending

Thank you for coming to today's seminar. As my gift to you, I would like to offer you a **20% discount off your order of *Special Needs in the General Classroom*.** Just select "Special Needs in the General Classroom" on the order form available at this seminar and include this coupon with your order, and you'll get your copy of the full book for just $19.97. ***Special Needs in the General Classroom*** offers a multitude of additional strategies, tips, and tools to enhance your experience in the inclusion classroom. Order your copy today!

Order Susan's Books!

Visit www.CogentCatalyst.com

CORWIN
A SAGE Company

RTI Strategies for Secondary Teachers

Susan Gingras Fitzell

A "strategy bank" for secondary teachers

Teachers want solutions, not theory. This book offers a bank of proven RTI strategies for Grades 6–12 that will improve test scores and student achievement for *all* students, not just struggling learners. Susan Gingras Fitzell explains how RTI fits into secondary education and applies it to math, reading comprehension, writing, and more. She summarizes tiers one, two, and three in teacher-friendly language and includes:

- Easily implemented and practical interventions
- Sample lesson plans and visual models
- Examples of how to address budgeting, staffing, performance, and student culture constraints

Table of Contents

July 2011, 152 pages, 8.5" x 11"
Paperback: **$29.95**, D11441-978-1-4129-9222-0

Back Cover

Made in the USA
San Bernardino, CA
28 May 2015